Adversity

to

Advantage

Adversity

to

Advantage

*3 Epic Stories of Transforming Life's
Obstacles into Opportunity*

Timothy Chhim

Tom Cunningham

Taylor Tagg

Adversity to Advantage: 3 Epic Stories of Transforming Life's

Obstacles into Opportunity

Copyright © 2015 Chhim, Cunningham, Tagg

All rights reserved.

PRAISE FOR ADVERSITY TO ADVANTAGE AND AUTHORS TIM CHHIM, TOM CUNNINGHAM, AND TAYLOR TAGG

"It is often difficult to comprehend why some people are faced with what may seem like insurmountable challenges while others are overwhelmed by the simple trials of day to day living. Having dealt with a plethora of devastating, life changing events, I admit that I often feared that I would never recover from Paralyses, Cancer, Bankruptcy and the impending death of my baby boy.

Today I live a most extraordinary life filled with gratitude for the trials I have faced. The beautiful truth is that we have all been equipped with the tools needed to rise from the ashes yet many lose sight of the amazing gifts on the other side of tragedy.

Tom, Timothy and Taylor have not only overcome tremendous obstacles, but they have found the true desire to help equip others with the tools needed to create a most beautiful life beyond the pain. Within these heartfelt stories you will find valuable nuggets of powerful inspiration to help you rise from the ashes and experience a reality that most people rarely dare to dream about.

Be prepared for a most emotional ride that will leave a mark on your heart for eternity. Beyond every great challenge awaits a greater Gift."

Savannah Ross, *RichMom*

"In my years as a social worker in the underprivileged east end of Glasgow, Scotland, I saw first-hand what adversity can do to people and families. I also witnessed people who lived positively through sometimes overwhelming challenges who were able to rise above their circumstances to serve others.

Napoleon Hill Foundation Certified Instructors Tim Chhim, Taylor Tagg, and Tom Cunningham share deeply personal stories of the adversities they have faced, as well as ideas and strategies to turn those challenges into opportunities to bless and serve others.

Napoleon Hill said that "Every adversity you meet carries with it a seed of equivalent or greater benefit." Adversity to Advantage will help you find your seed of equivalent benefit so that you can turn your adversities into advantages that will serve you and others."

Jack Black, Founder of Mindstore International, Mindstore.com

"Beyond doubt, three astonishing true stories that will emotionally move and inspire you. These stories about survival, chronic pain, and overcoming fear prove that anyone can turn Adversity into Advantage if they believe they can."

Jeremy Rayzor, Co-Founder of Rayzor Sharp Entertainment Inc, Rayzorsharpent.com

"In the inspiring new book from Tom, Taylor, and Timothy you get an up close look at how three men turned intense challenges into inspiration for thousands of others. We will ALL face challenges. Many people will let it stop them and suppress their true inner genius. A few will get stronger from it. Let these three agents of positive change give you the gift of their stories, wisdom, and perspective in this amazing book."

Tony Rubleski, Creator, *Mind Capture Group.com*

"Every story I've ever read about a life success has always started with some form of adversity. There are those that resign themselves to letting it hold them back. These three guys chose to stand up and be counted, and created their new and improved lives. Congratulations to Tom Cunningham (too tall), Timothy Chhim and Taylor Tagg for not only making new lives for themselves, but also on sharing their intimate stories with the world."

Peter Goral, *Art Envy.faso.com*

"It's not often you come across a body of work that inspires you to look at life and its offerings all over again. Adversity to Advantage is a wonderfully written motivational book of 3 incredible stories and life experiences that do just that! Get ready to embark on a journey of self discovery, reflection and appreciation of life itself. If you've ever felt as if you've not had a fair chance to succeed in life, then this book is a MUST READ!"

Yoni Ashurov, President, CEO of *MWR Life.com*

"Tom, Tim, and Taylor have heroically gifted their stories of adversity for the benefit of others. The lessons gained here are priceless."

Jimmy Burgess, Founder of *BeMoreUniversity.com*

"If you are looking for a guidebook on courage, determination and survival, Adversity to Advantage is the book for you. The three authors; Timothy Chhim, Tom Cunningham and Taylor Tagg lay bare before us their amazing, true-life experiences, revealing life's higher purpose. In a day and age when stardom is based on posing for a selfie, this book is a breath of authenticity."

Brad Szollose, Author of *Liquid Leadership, BradSzollose.com*

DEDICATION

Dedicated with love to my father, who died without knowing where I was; to my mother, who believed I would survive; and to my sisters, who sacrificed their opportunities for me. And to the millions of innocent Khmers who were killed and injured in Cambodia's war and through the atrocities of the Pol Pot regime.

Timothy Chhim

To everyone who is living positively through the many and varied challenges of life.

Tom Cunningham

To those struggling for hope, may you find some here.

Taylor Tagg

CONTENTS

ACKNOWLEDGMENTS

Timothy Chhim

My deepest appreciation goes first to my family. To my wife, Neang, we have gone through many obstacles to achieve our dream of freedom for ourselves and for our children. I would like to thank you for your unending support throughout my journey of writing this book and touring around the country to enlighten others.

To my eldest daughter, Rojana, you have been an integral part of helping me keep the family business intact and running smoothly; I couldn't have done it without you.

To my second daughter, Suzy, you have been my first editor since I started my first draft of my story. Thank you for taking the time to read my story and giving me your opinions on how to make my story come to life.

To my son, Tony, you are the product that despite having difficulties in life, one is able to overcome and come up on top; I am proud of you.

I also would like to thank my co-authors, Tom Cunningham and Taylor Tagg, for their constant encouragement and patience. Your stories and words have greatly influenced me and I am so grateful that our paths have crossed.

Last, I would like to give thanks to our editor, Loria Kulathugam, who helped shaped my words to make them into a story that you, the reader, are able to understand and enjoy to the fullest.

Tom Cunningham

Like many people, who I am is a reflection of two women in my life: my mom, Lynda Appleby, and my wife, Kim Cunningham. They have lived with and through my health challenges due to a severe case of rheumatoid arthritis.

My mother has suffered as much, or more, than I have in taking care of my painful and debilitating joints. My wife knows all the numerous challenges I encounter in a regular day, and she helps me to overcome them. I am who I am because of my mom and Kim.

Many of my most enjoyable childhood memories, and throughout my life, are the times I spent with my dad. We did all the things that boys dream of doing and those memories are ones I regularly revisit. My dad and I played road hockey, ice hockey, baseball, golf, cards, and attended Montreal Canadiens, Montreal Expos and Montreal Alouette games. I cherish the time I spend with my dad. My father and I still enjoy spending time together over a drink and a game of cribbage.

My sisters, Lorraine and Sarah, are two of the many blessings that God has given me. Their early years were taken up with visiting me in hospitals and having my parents focus their time and attention on me. We fought and disagreed like all siblings, but they were always there to help me in whatever ways they could.

The Bible refers to the type of friend ". . . who sticks closer than a brother" in Proverbs 18:24. I am fortunate to have two such friends, who have been there with me in good times and bad: Chris Sernoskie and Keith Bodger. Although they are well aware, from over 35 years of friendship, of the severity of my health challenges, both know when and how to help me when I need it and when and how to let me be myself and not treat me any differently than they would anyone else.

The thing that excites me the most in my life now is being a Napoleon Hill Foundation Certified Instructor. I feel smarter and taller when I tell people about it. The people I have befriended through association with this organization enrich my life and help me pursue my God-given purpose of encouraging others to live positively through the many and varied challenges of life.

I cannot mention everybody, however, I have to specifically name Judy Williamson, Don Green, Uriel Martinez (Chino), Alan Chen, and Pat and Livio Andreatta. I hold all of them in very high regard and sometimes have to pinch myself when I communicate directly with them.

Taylor Tagg

I would first like to thank my wife Sherri for her unending love and support for me. Your beauty inside and out stuns me every single day.

I also thank my mom, Patsy Stairs, and dad, Billy Tagg. Without your love, support, and examples, both positive and negative, I could not have learned what I needed to become the man I am today. Thank you, mom and dad, from the bottom of my heart. I love you both with all that I am.

I would also like to thank my heroes in life, my grandparents, Edwin and Sarah Hughes, who taught me how to love unconditionally. I hope to become as loving to others as you were to me.

Furthermore, I would like to thank Dr. Napoleon Hill, whose voice changed the course of my life in an instant. Dr. Hill reassured me that nothing in life was for naught and every single difficulty carried with it an equal benefit if I was willing to find it.

Not a day has gone by since I heard those words many years ago, that I haven't put that natural law to use in my life. My soul will always be grateful for that enduring lesson.

To all those who have yet to discover that everything in our lives, both good and bad, is meant for us to move through in order to grow, I send you my love and peace for the journey to success ahead. Godspeed brothers and sisters.

Lastly, a special heartfelt thanks goes to Joy Jacoway and Loria Kulathugam for bringing this book to life. Joy gave us the courage early on to keep persevering when this book seemed in doubt, and Loria brought the light into Adversity to Advantage that is still shining today. Thank you both for your contributions and hard work. I am forever grateful.

FOREWORD

I have just finished reading *Adversity to Advantage: 3 Epic Stories of Transforming Life's Obstacles into Opportunity* by Timothy Chhim, Tom Cunningham, and Taylor Tagg.

I am humbled by the immensity of the suffering that all three have experienced in their lives, and I am impressed by their willingness to share and relate these stories to their readers. I know each author personally since they have been students of mine.

Many memories exist of them in class and also as speakers. I have seen each of them struggle emotionally as their stories were told to groups, and how the audience responded. They share these episodes from their lives not to impress us, but to inspire us to follow in their footsteps because if one of us can learn from their formula for success, we all can.

They write because they love.

Tim Chhim told me his story in a restaurant in Ireland. I was stunned and found it hard to imagine that anyone who experienced the inhumanity that he did could be so objective in sharing his thoughts. I marveled at his comeback and persistence in yet working to better himself.

My thoughts stayed with him in Cambodia as I relived the Vietnam War and its spread to surrounding countries. It was an ugly time, and I marveled that someone could arrive on the other side of the conflict and still be focused on living positively in a free world. His definiteness of purpose never faltered, and he survived to tell about achieving his goal.

Was he unharmed? No.

Tim endured and survived with grace intact, and today he uses that grace to share his belief that a better life is achievable if you keep your desire directly in front of your immediate vision. Tim serves as a lighthouse whose beam can direct others to freedom of body, mind, and spirit.

Tom Cunningham is a person I admire and think about daily since being introduced to him by a mutual friend, Shane Morand. Shane himself treasured Tom's friendship so much that he asked me to consider him for a speaking engagement at our annual Open House for the Napoleon Hill World Learning Center at Purdue University Calumet.

Shane made the introductions and Tom did the rest. Not only did he show up and present his speech, but he also showed up driving himself all the way from Canada, making no excuses about how difficult that must have been for him. His talk regarding learning from adversity and defeat captivated the audience.

I never considered not putting him on the platform again.

Tom's natural speaking ability plus his desire to influence and help people who need healing are sincere and the main reasons that people associate the word AMAZING with Tom. He programs it into everyone's mind that he is indeed amazing and an advanced practitioner of Dr. Hill's Science of Success Philosophy.

In physique, Tom may not be "too tall," but in the eyes of those that love him and support him, he is an amazing giant to behold. Because Tom shows us that he can, we are caught in his enthusiasm and know that we can too!

I first met Taylor Tagg as he traveled with his mother to join the Leader Certification Class in Ireland. Taylor is quiet and contemplative but never misses a beat as to what is going on around him. He takes it all in and mulls everything over in his mind prior to seeing if what is being presented works for him or not.

I could sense many inner thoughts and feelings flaring up inside of Taylor as he listened and sometimes discussed his breaking out of a cycle of abuse. His desire was to share what had happened to him so that others would know how not to become a victim, but a victor on the other side of negative experiences.

Through thinking, discussion, journaling, and writing, Taylor discovered several unique processes that enabled him and now others to travel through fears and "dark nights" to find the benefit in the adversity. His techniques are excellent examples of how to heal yourself and replace anger and hate, with forgiveness and love.

Taylor has positioned himself as a leader in the process of learning from adversity and defeat. He teaches us the difference one little seemingly inconsequential word can make in bringing us through the fear that can stop us in our tracks. Find out how changing only one word can guide us to the place of healing at a peaceful pace.

That, itself, is a kernel of wisdom in his story!

This book is short and can be finished in one sitting. But, the thoughts, comments, and suggestions of all three authors stay with you for a long time.

Be willing to travel through Tim's early life in Cambodia, Tom's struggles with illness since the age of five, and Taylor's fears as he grabbed them by the tail and never let go.

All reach into our psyches and prepare us to transform our life's adversities.

There is a simple prayer, called the ***Prayer of St. Francis*** that comes to mind when I consider the purpose of this book. It reads as follows:

Lord, make me an instrument of thy peace.

Where there is hatred, let me sow love,

Where there is injury, pardon;

Where there is doubt, faith;

Where there is despair, hope;

Where there is darkness, light;

And where there is sadness, joy.

O Divine Master, grant that I may not so much seek

To be consoled as to console,

To be understood as to understand,

To be loved, as to love.

For it is in giving that we receive,

It is in pardoning that we are pardoned,

And it is in dying that we are born to eternal life.

-- St. Francis of Assisi

I challenge you to read this book with the above prayer in mind, and see how many times Tim, Tom, and Taylor use the pattern of St. Francis' formula in their healing.

I am certain you will find multiple examples from each of their stories that will demonstrate explicitly how our authors sow love, pardon, faith, hope, light, and joy in all circumstances.

Their purpose is to console, understand, and love those they encounter as the true stepping-stones to enduring peace.

What better recipe is there in overcoming adversity than making the world a better place in which to live? Allow Tim, Tom, and Taylor to lead you to a better way in this process for yourself and others.

I highly recommend *Adversity to Advantage* for the peace and understanding that it will bring to you now and the times when you may need it the most.

Judith Williamson

Director: Napoleon Hill World Learning Center

Purdue University Calumet

INTRODUCTION

"Once the storm is over, you won't remember
how you made it through, how you managed to
survive. You won't even be sure whether the storm
is really over. But one thing is certain. When you
come out of the storm, you won't be the same
person who walked in. That's what this storm's all
about."

Haruki Murakami, *Hard-Boiled Wonderland
and the End of the World*

Have you weathered a storm you were not certain you could endure?

Can you spot darkened clouds on your horizon even now?

The tempests shared in this book are honest and compelling. Three men chronicle their unique journeys through challenges and pain. While their obstacles are varied, their responses reflect a common thread of hope and survival on their journeys to success.

In John C. Maxwell's book, *Your Road Map for Success*, he defines success as "knowing your purpose in life, growing to reach your maximum potential, and sowing seeds that benefit others." He suggests that "one of the major keys to success is to keep moving forward on the journey, making the best of the detours and interruptions, turning adversity into advantage."

Rather than adopting the stance of victims, these authors all journey toward this definition of success by facing their individual challenges head-on.

For the first time, Tim unveils his story on these pages. Born in Cambodia, he grew up in desperate poverty. Yet he managed to maintain optimism during childhood by drawing on a vivid imagination. Tim's parents sacrificed everything to ensure his education and future.

Sent away to a school at ten, he served like a slave in a monastery where he felt lonely being separated from his loving family.

With sheer determination, he continued to overcome obstacles and accomplished the incredible goal of completing high school. Then the political turmoil of Cambodia dreadfully traumatized his life with unspeakable violence.

Tim's gripping journey includes narrowly escaping death several times and losing many he loved.

Tom shares his personal story with chronic pain. Contending with rheumatoid arthritis from a young age resulted in numerous surgeries and prolonged recoveries. He relays the challenges of never being pain free in spite of medical intervention. Although typically positive, Tom is authentic about facing deep loss and battling depression.

However, rather than allow himself to question why he has such extreme physical challenges, he asks,

"How can I be the best I can despite the situation?"

And he intentionally focuses on how to use this adversity to help others. A key to gaining this remarkable perspective has been continually reading inspiring stories of those who have made positive contributions in spite of significant challenges.

While processing his abuse as a child, Taylor came to a pivotal shift in thinking about feeling defeated. His realization that defeat can serve as an instructor, allowed him to productively process two more recent challenges. The first came in his professional role when he chose to face a devastating error with openness and integrity.

The second came when he bravely overcame his paralyzing fear of public speaking. He challenges us to shift our thinking from things happening *to* us to things happening *for* us.

Focusing on his audience rather than himself, he sets out a blueprint for living that can empower us all. His desire is evident for others to move forward from being stuck or defeated.

In his final chapter he walks through four questions to analyze approaches to adversity.

These men could easily have been overwhelmed by tragedy. Or bitter at being thrown into such tumultuous storms. But rather than perceive their stories as unwelcome tragedies, they chose to process them as life-changing opportunities.

In his book *Where is God When it Hurts*, author Philip Yancey states there are four "frontiers where every suffering person will do battle: fear, helplessness, meaning and hope. Our response to suffering depends largely on the outcome of our struggle in those frontiers."

Tim, Tom, and Taylor willingly share their stories of suffering with us, and reflect the truth of Yancey's quote. Although facing different enemies, their journeys have a common thread of struggling with fear and helplessness.

And perhaps writing this book together symbolizes taking another step on their journey towards finding the meaning and hope they long for.

These are their stories of adversity to advantage.

These are our stories of adversity to advantage.

All are welcome.

A JOURNEY
TO
FREEDOM:

Tim Chhim's Story

1

A JOURNEY TO FREEDOM:
Timothy Chhim's Story

When my children were young, during holiday seasons and especially at Christmas time, they often asked me why they never received presents from their grandparents, uncles and aunts, cousins, or other relatives.

To this day, their voices echo in my ears: "Daddy, how come we don't have any gifts from our grandpas or grandmas?" Sometimes, they wept and innocently asked: "Where are they, daddy? Why don't we have any relatives?"

Over the years, I have learned to cope with tears, but it has been difficult to hide my emotions of love and compassion and sorrow when asked questions like these. It has been even harder to hold back the stories of my background in fear that I would somehow cause trauma to their hearts and minds.

Nevertheless, I knew that one day I would reveal my true story to my children and to others—the ordeal of my family and my country. That day has come and I now share this powerful story with them and with the world.

The Innocent Years

During my early years, surrounded by poverty, I knew nothing about prosperity or happiness. However, I experienced recurring dreams of hope that I could change my life. I didn't know how it was possible, but I was convinced I could.

I was born into an impoverished family, the youngest of five siblings. In the years before I started school, I seldom saw my four sisters or my parents. They left for their back-breaking work in the rice fields before dawn and returned home after dark. When they came home in the evening, they would continue working until midnight at a second job, hand-weaving utility baskets.

Preschool or kindergarten did not exist, so when my parents and sisters were busy in the rice paddy fields, I was often left at home, unattended. I played with other children in the nearby rice fields: chasing after butterflies, catching lizards on white sand, and looking for live frogs and snakes in swampy ponds. Sometimes my mother would carry me on her waist or on her back to the paddy fields; that was where I was taught to work.

During my primary school years in the early 1960s, although Cambodia was at peace, it was among the poorest nations on earth. I had no idea that an outside world existed. Children in remote villages, including mine, attended school many kilometers away from home. We walked to school, barefoot, three to four hours a day for five days a week regardless of the weather conditions.

Every morning, my alarm clock was the crowing of roosters or the squeaky noises of the villagers' oxcarts as they left for work. My mother was an additional wakeup caller. After preparing our lunch, she would throw a pillow at us if we failed to get up right away.

I loved the smell of her freshly-cooked rice and roasted salty fish that filled the morning air, as she cooked over the fire in our dilapidated kitchen with palm-leaf walls.

I rarely heard or saw my father—a religious man, who had lost his right eye in the First Indo-China War. He was quiet, but the most respected member of our family. He listened more than he talked. He was a dedicated Buddhist and spent most of his free time at a small monastery in the forest to the east of our home. He usually left for the rice fields before the roosters crowed.

My four older sisters had very little schooling as they had to work to help support the family. My youngest sister, Salom, was 7 years older than I was and Senn was a few years older than her. My two oldest sisters were married and lived in the same village.

My sisters often encouraged me, saying that they would rather be ignorant so that I could be educated. They believed that a boy should have more opportunity to learn than a girl.

I was the youngest and smallest child in my class, but I did better than most students. I liked to compete against the older students, and worked even harder because of my small size. Primary schooling was available for all ages, including children who had not started school on time.

Some of my classmates were teenagers, and they often bullied the younger children by hitting and teasing them for fun. They did not like to see the smallest child outwork them; so I made up my mind to surpass them. Teachers were extremely strict and even violent. They whipped students with rattan sticks or punished them if homework was not done or if wrong answers were given. I was fearful of the bullies, as well as the teachers, but I conquered my fears through faith, dreams, and hard work. I believed that if I overcame these challenges, my life would be better in the future. I have kept those childhood dreams alive ever since.

Small Yet Powerful Dreams

Dreaming was one of my favorite ways to keep my mind occupied during the long walk to and from school each day. I wished that I could fly and soar like the hawks and eagles I saw roaming the blue sky.

Every now and then, I would stretch out my arms and pretend that they were wings and start flapping to take off while running along the dirt road. I realized I was not up in the air, but I could get to my destination faster with such an imagination.

On other days, I visualized that I had a small bicycle so I could get to school more quickly and avoid being punished. I would reach out both of my arms, pretending to steer a shiny, blue bike. If I was late for school, my dream became more elaborate.

I imagined I had a red sports car to speed along beside muddy rice fields, waving at all the bullies and the houses in the village as I passed by. To make my dream more realistic, I would close my lips firmly and force the air out of my mouth to make it sound like a car's engine, "broom… broom…broom," and then start running as fast as I could with both hands in the air, steering the wheel in different directions.

I dreamed that one day, instead of playing with a tin sardine can and coconut shells, I would have better toys than the richest kids in my class. While running along the dikes between rice paddies, I never took my eyes off the pathways in the hope that I would find some abandoned toys or even some money on the ground.

I planned to sell the toys and use the money to purchase candy to sell to my richer schoolmates. I would use the profits to buy new clothes since with new, clean clothes I could play with other kids and be accepted by the girls I admired. Yes, with new, clean clothes I was sure that those girls would not look down on me ever again.

My dreams also included better food. On my way home from school, knowing there was only rice and dried fish for dinner, I imagined there was a feast of many hot dishes waiting for me, along with fresh, clean water to drink. I had no idea how my imaginary food would taste, but imagining all that "made-in-heaven food" made my dried fish taste much better.

If I got caught in a heavy monsoon rainstorm, I would pretend that the sound of raindrops against my face, the rumbles of thunder, and the flashes of lightning that echoed through the jungle were the beautiful sounds of music to my ears. I felt I was never alone and envisioned that there was always a good friend walking or running beside me, protecting me.

During the monsoon, the rain fell with such strength on my face, ears, and bare shoulders that it made my lips vibrate and numbed my face. I imagined the pain to be nothing more than the soft fingers of a girlfriend or of my mother trying to comfort me. I dreamed that one day I would be free from hunger, cold, and loneliness.

Walking alone to and from school also made me love and appreciate my older sisters even more, as when they were with me, they would shield me from the rain or the sun and keep me warm and safe.

Overcoming Obstacles from Within

Monsoon rains and storms were not the only obstacles I faced; there was also a mysterious group known as *Pramatt Pramang*, as well as wild animals that lived in the jungle.

Our elders warned us that *Pramatt Pramang* was vicious. This group kidnapped hundreds of young children and took them to North Vietnam to train them to become communist. I was told that North Vietnam and South Vietnam were at war. I didn't know what war was, but on quiet days, I could hear the far-off rumbling sound of gunfire to the east: the sounds of fighting in Vietnam. I hoped the war did not spill over into Cambodia.

When other children tried to frighten me with stories of wild animals, I turned my fears into faith. I could see tigers, wild boars, wolves, and other wild animals roaming the forests nearby. Instead of being fearful, I imagined that those animals were my friends who would protect me from the *Pramatt Pramang*.

I spent three years of elementary school learning how to cope with schoolwork, homework, and household chores to help my family survive. Other kids made fun of me because I had to bring our family's cattle—bulls and cows—to school to care for them. I fed them grass on the way to and from school, tied them up in the empty field near my school, and checked on them whenever we had a break.

This helped free up my parents so they could be more productive on our farmland. I was kind and friendly to our animals and they kept me company. One young bull, named *ah Pich* or Diamond, became my personal pet and my mode of luxury transportation.

He was the only one who allowed me to ride on his back. He became my imaginary black Citroën, the beautiful car I saw at a Buddhist temple during a New Year ceremony.

Turning Shame into Hope

It was a hot and dry April. Many people came from the city to our rural village to celebrate the Cambodian New Year. There were only a few cars parked on the grass under the shade trees in my village.

One was an elegant black Citroën—a French-made car—that was clean and shiny and smelled wonderful. I could see my own reflection on the door: a small barefoot boy, wearing only black torn and mud-stained shorts.

"What a beautiful machine!" I exclaimed quietly.

I was fascinated, and desperately wanted to touch the car, but didn't dare. I moved slowly toward the car to look again at my reflection in the side door, when suddenly . . .

"Get away from my car, and don't touch it! Get away! If you don't, I'll tell my father to beat you up!"

My heart raced. I jumped back from the car and turned around. A young girl, about my age, stood a few feet behind me with her hands on her hips, eyes opened wide, angrily yelling as if I was going to damage or steal her most precious property. I was humiliated, ashamed, and speechless.

I knew by looking at her that her clothes were nicer than any I had seen in my village, and she was much cleaner than I was. I doubted that she was as kind as I, though. I did not look her in the eyes for long, and I slowly walked away from the vehicle.

Deep within, I promised myself that when I grew up, I would own a much nicer car than that Citroën. From then on, I dreamed that someday I would drive my very own car, and in the meantime, *ah Pich*, my little bull without horns, was my vehicle.

This incident made me realize that I must do something to fight poverty and be free from fear.

From Dog to Discipline

In 1964, at the age of ten, my parents sent me away to complete the second part of primary school (grades four to seven). One hot day, my parents brought me to a Buddhist temple about five kilometers away from home.

They appealed to the chief monk, or abbot, to allow me to stay in the temple so I could attend the school located in the temple grounds. I would become a "pagoda boy." My father gave the abbot permission to do whatever he wanted to make sure I succeeded in school.

He said that he only wanted my bones and skin back; the rest of me belonged to the monk. I was frightened as it was the first time I was away from my home and family. The abbot and his monks were extremely strict and occasionally violent.

As one of the pagoda boys, I was only allowed to return home a few times per year. The route to my village led through the middle of a jungle, filled with many wild animals, giving me nightmares that continue even now.

Life in the pagoda was difficult. Children who were accepted as pagoda boys had to work hard and serve the monks like slaves. In addition, people in the nearby villages, my classmates among them, considered pagoda boys to be nothing but parasites.

They often called us "pagoda dogs" because we ate the leftovers from the monks' meals. I had no other choice but to succeed for I could never return home if I failed. I worked hard, endured much, and turned those three long years into my temple of personal discipline in order to outwork, outlearn, and outdo most of my peers at the temple and at school.

Life without parents at this young age was very painful. I longed to see my parents and sisters. I wanted to be with them and feel their love. My parents rarely came to see me at the temple, and when they came to visit, they spent most of their time with the abbot.

Although I knew that they loved me dearly, I felt neglected. Nevertheless, I was able to move from being a "dog of the Temple" to become a boy of discipline.

The Next Adventure: High School

In 1967, only six out of the 50 students in my school passed the examination to enter high school. Three of the six were the "pagoda dogs." All the bullies I knew were left behind, and I triumphantly returned home for the summer.

The people of my village were proud of my great achievement and I received many hugs and kisses. However, my parents were faced with another major problem. They could not afford the fees for my high school tuition, dormitory accommodation, and transportation. I thought my dream of high school was destroyed.

Instead, my parents sold most of their farmland to support my education. I had to leave home for the second time. It was much farther than before as the only high school in my province was in the provincial capital, about 15 kilometers away.

For the first three years, I drifted from place to place in order to live close to the school. I lived with my parents' friend as a houseboy. I also lived with friends and strangers in small shacks in people's backyards. Then I became a pagoda boy again—once more a "pagoda dog."

I had no way to go home. A few times a year, my parents came to visit me. I was moved when I saw that my mother had brought coins and old bills—their life savings— for my books and school supplies. Since beginning high school, I had not seen my sisters or other relatives. I saw them in my mind as I recalled memories of our childhood.

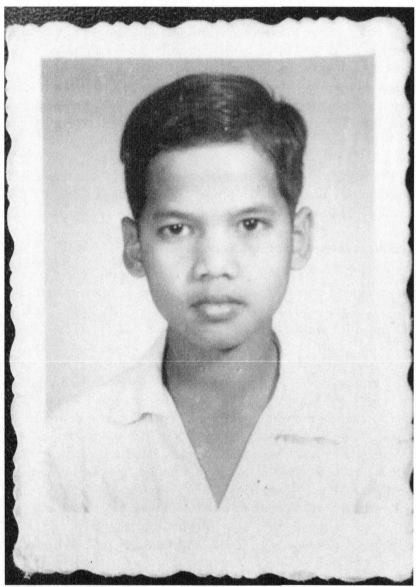

Tim as a "pagoda dog" in 6th grade

War Comes to Cambodia

The war I feared came to Cambodia on March 18, 1970, when Cambodia was caught up in the Vietnam War. The government, under the leadership of General Lon Nol, overthrew the Head of State, Prince Norodom Sihanouk, in a coup. Later that year, it established Cambodia as the Khmer Republic, and the government declared war against the Viet Cong and North Vietnamese forces that were hidden inside Cambodian territory, fighting against the South Vietnamese and the Americans.

The prince, now in Beijing, broadcast a message asking his subjects to rise up against the new American-backed Lon Nol government. Many Cambodians, including most people in my village, joined the prince, who later allied himself with his former enemy, the Khmer Rouge. They were assisted by the Viet Cong and North Vietnamese and supported by China and the Soviet Union.

The new government of the Khmer Republic, on the other hand, asked the people to fight against the intruders to help protect their liberty and rights. They wanted to prevent the return of "monarchical government."

The country was split over these events, including my family and millions of others. I went home from school for a few weeks. My family and I had differing opinions about the political situation in Cambodia.

My mother and sisters opposed the overthrow of the prince. My father considered both positions and took no sides. He gave us the opportunity to think for ourselves. I felt caught in the middle.

With the information I had learned in school, I passionately opposed the prince's policies that allowed the North Vietnamese and Viet Cong forces to hide in and use Cambodian territory. I shared the new government's policies and decided that I would do what I could to help the Khmer Republic.

Many uneducated peasants joined the prince and Khmer Rouge, and participated in demonstrations and riots, but most high school and university students supported the new government. I joined the government forces and became one of the student fighters known as "Commandos."

I remember noticing that my gun was taller than I was.

Surprisingly, the Viet Cong attacked my school in June that year, which convinced me that they meant business. When I returned home to let my parents know I was safe, my father suggested that I become a Buddhist monk to avoid being sent to the battle zones.

I became a novice monk at the same temple I had stayed in as a pagoda boy during my primary school years. When the communists gained strength in that area, the abbot sent me away to continue my Buddhist education in a different district. Nearly a year later, I decided to leave monkhood to rejoin my high school.

The Commando

The war continued and intensified fiercely. American bombings of Khmer Rouge positions were heard, seen, and felt many times during the day and night. My entire village and many others were destroyed by the air raids. My parents and my sisters and their families were displaced by the bombing.

By this time, more poor peasants had left their homes to join the Khmer Rouge and Prince Sihanouk to fight against the Lon Nol government. I learned later that they would succeed in their quest, but at the time, I refused to believe.

I went back to high school, not just to study, but to train to fight as well. Some students quit school and joined the army but many, like me, chose to enroll in "Student Commando teams" in response to calls by the government. We studied during the day and fought by night.

The government provided only a meager salary for Student Commandos, and I survived with the help of a few friends, monks, and schoolmates who provided small donations of food.

I didn't have a chance to say goodbye to my family and friends when I returned to high school, and deep inside I felt that I would never see them again. I could not go back home because, by that time, communist forces dominated my hometown.

I never did see my family again, with the exception of my father, who one day risked his life to come to my school to bring me some rice and money. We hugged and cried. He told me to be careful and left me with these words, pertaining to Cambodian political issues. He said to me: "One side is likened to eagles, and the other side is likened to tigers, only a wise person can choose the right one." He hugged me so tight I could hardly breathe, and looked at me straight in my eyes as he continued:

"Goodbye, my only son, and remember that your mother and I will always love you."

I didn't know what he meant by his words about the political situation, and I still don't. I hoped that one day when the war ended we could discuss it.

That day never came, for I learned afterward that my father died from food poisoning in 1972.

Some people speculated that he was poisoned for political reasons. I felt numb and wept silently, without tears.

I was in shock—confused and angry. I resolved to turn the pain into faith that one day Cambodia would be free and I would be able to return home.

As a Student Commando, I fought alongside the Cambodian Army against the well-equipped and experienced Viet Cong and North Vietnamese forces, and the Khmer Rouge. Later, the Khmer Rouge seemed to take charge in most battles, which led many people to believe that the war in Cambodia was a "civil war."

Cambodians fought each other viciously with hatred, revenge, and fear. Many of my friends and schoolmates were killed in front of my eyes.

Seeking Freedom

In 1973, at the age of 18, I finished high school. I developed a bigger and better dream: I knew I had to seek freedom—the freedom from fear, hunger, and oppression of body and mind. In just three short years I had seen so much destruction of human lives, property, natural resources, and almost all societal and economic infrastructures within Cambodia. I decided I would go to the capital city of Phnom Penh to look for work and further my education.

All highways leading to Phnom Penh had been cut off by Khmer Rouge soldiers, and it was very expensive to fly from my province. For many days I searched for ways and means to travel, until finally this dream came true.

A friend, who had connections with a military officer, got me a flight to Phnom Penh in a military plane. I sold most of my clothing, pots and pans, and other belongings to pay for the thirty-minute flight on a twin-propeller plane that transported military equipment and pigs. The pilot seated me on the floor with the pigs, who were all loudly squealing inside their small bamboo cages.

I realized then that pigs could fly!

I searched for work in the capital for some time, until I found one of my uncles, who invited me to stay with his family. I later got a job as a Republican police officer, while attending university in the evening. My dream of freedom was always on my mind.

Meanwhile, the war continued. Phnom Penh was isolated from other provinces and the cost of living in the city skyrocketed. At the beginning of 1975, the communist troops tightened their noose around Phnom Penh and the other provincial capitals.

The Khmer Rouge troops moved closer to the capital and fired rockets and artillery shells on a daily basis. Many people died in the explosions. Schools and businesses were interrupted constantly. I began to wonder if the government could survive. I realized that people had lost confidence in the Lon Nol government and in American aid and support. Everyone began to prepare for the worst, and many wealthy families left the country.

I saw so much suffering and brutality on a daily basis as I traveled to and from school. People were killed or injured right in front of me by rocket explosions.

Sometimes, the blasts came so close that I was forced to dash to safety. Cambodian blood was spilled all over the city. Indeed, the sights, the sounds, and the smells of the explosions are still etched in my memory.

The Fall of Phnom Penh

On April 14, 1975, I was stationed in Ta Khmao, a small town south of Phnom Penh, to help guard the governor's office in my role as a Republican police officer. I saw hundreds of Khmer Rouge soldiers on the east side of the Mekong River, shelling the town nonstop. People in the town were frightened, and began packing up and fleeing Ta Khmao toward Phnom Penh.

I also fled for safety.

The Khmer Rouge had captured many bases close to the capital, and continued to attack various areas of the city with more and more shells and rockets. Many people were injured and killed. I could clearly hear the final battles being fought all around the capital. We could not sleep and were dreadfully scared.

With the aid of the North Vietnamese and the Viet Cong, and using the mountains of southern Cambodia as their retreat, the Khmer Rouge carried on a systematic war against the government. Despite massive economic and military aid from the United

States—including bombing of Khmer Rouge positions—the Lon Nol government continued to lose territory to the communist troops. Phnom Penh, the capital, finally fell to the Khmer Rouge on April 17, 1975.

On the morning of that historic day, I joined the throngs of people who stood along the sidewalks outside their homes, waving white flags to welcome the young Khmer Rouge soldiers. People piled their personal guns and other weapons in front of their homes to be collected by the victorious Khmer Rouge.

The soldiers, wearing ragged black pajamas and Maoist caps, waved back as they walked in an orderly fashion along the streets. Most of them were covered with mud. They looked pale and weak, and carried AK-47s and other weapons.

Everyone was relieved that peace had finally arrived and hoped that it would prevail. I lifted up one of my young nieces and told her the war was over and everything would now be safe.

Nevertheless, I realized deep down that my hope for freedom was now in vain, because the communists had won the war.

I had no idea what I would do, and it seemed that my dreams of freedom were dead.

The Exodus

A communist government under the Khmer Rouge dictator, Pol Pot, was established. The new regime immediately implemented a program of radical social change. The entire population of Phnom Penh, along with other towns and cities across Cambodia, was evacuated to rural areas.

We were told to leave the city at once. All eight of us—my uncle and his wife, their 20-year-old daughter and her fiancé, 13-year-old daughter, two sons aged 16 and 10, and I—were shocked and close to tears.

We did not want to leave, but death was the only alternative. Those who refused to leave were killed on the spot and we witnessed many such incidents.

We waited until April 19 before departing. We carried enough food and supplies to last several days, as we had been instructed by the soldiers.

For several days, we walked north under the steamy hot sun along National Highway 5, leading to rural areas. It was a slow

45

journey, as the highway was very crowded and congested with thousands of people leaving the capital.

I could see and smell the decaying bodies of dead soldiers and war victims, covered by swarms of flies, lying beside the highway. Many bodies lay on the highway itself, and we had to jump over them in order to move ahead.

Along with thousands of others, we had to prepare food, eat, and sleep wherever we could find an empty space. We rested on walkways, along the riverbank, in the woods, in the open fields, and under trees. Many people were killed or injured by landmines and other explosive devices.

After travelling for a week, we were approximately 15 miles north of the capital. By this time, we had run out of food, and we all began to feel sick and weak. People began to leave unnecessary items they could no longer carry.

Money was abolished and could no longer be used anywhere in the country. Khmer Rouge officials set up food stations along the trails, but there were not enough for the vast numbers of people. To help supplement the basic food given by officials, we searched for food on our own. We tried to catch fish and collect shellfish from the Mekong River.

Love Not Meant to Be

At one point during this long journey I became so ill that I could barely walk. I asked my uncle to leave me and continue on with his family, but he refused and insisted that I travel with them.

During the second week of our march to the unknown, we met the family of my uncle's next-door neighbor, and they joined us in our journey. It was a blessed moment for me, because their daughter, Sopheap, was a girl I dreamed of marrying someday.

About three weeks into our journey, the new government officials set up many roadblocks in order to collect each traveller's personal information. We were instructed to return to our original village or to the place of our family origin. That was our last day with Sopheap's family, and my dream of being with Sopheap also died.

Sopheap's family had to travel to the southern part of the country and I had to return to my original province in the north. Sopheap and I went to catch some fresh water prawns on our last day together. She wanted to come with me to my hometown, and I agreed, but only if her parents did not object.

Her parents rejected her request and were upset. They wanted us to get married first, but that was impossible under the circumstances. They also claimed I could not support her, and we understood their decision.

Sopheap and I sat down and talked in the light rain just before we were separated. She was shaking and crying. She hugged me for the first and the last time and said:

"Brother, when we return to the Capital one day, we will then get married."

She smiled through her tears and continued: "I will always wait for you, and please remember that I will always love you."

I couldn't talk.

I kissed her for the first and last time on her right cheek.

We waved good-bye to each other until we were out of sight.

I never heard from her or saw her again.

Death Row and Renewed Dreams

The following day, we were stopped again at the next roadblock. The officials grouped my uncle's family with others who had served in the Khmer Republican military services. We were housed at a Buddhist temple for the night, and in the morning, armed soldiers escorted all of us to a remote village.

We continued to be moved to different areas over the next few days; eventually being placed in a closely-guarded camp called Manteay Chass, about 10 kilometers away from the main highway.

The conditions of the makeshift campground in the middle of a rice field were horrible, with no water supply and insufficient food. My cousins and I built a small sleeping shelter out of pieces of wood and brush.

A few days later, village officials arrived with a list of eighty-eight families who would leave the camp to return to the Capital in order to help rebuild the country and to receive Prince Sihanouk. My name was on the list, but my uncle and his family were not.

We were told not to bring much with us, and were escorted by armed soldiers to an old Buddhist Temple about six kilometers away. We were all joyful and happy at the prospect of returning to the Capital.

During that trip, I met an old acquaintance. He told me he had just escaped from a killing site after he too had been told to go back to Phnom Penh to help rebuild the country and receive the prince.

"It was not true," he said. He showed me a deep wound on the back of his head as proof. He begged me to run: "My friend," he whispered, "you are being sent to be executed, you must escape!"

I didn't fully believe him until I got to the temple and was alerted by two sympathetic villagers—an old cow herder and a mysterious pale woman. With different clues, they told me that the temple was used as a transit point to the killing site near the mountain. I began to plan my escape, but I dared not reveal it to anyone else.

I wanted to depart at night but we were closely guarded by armed soldiers. I tried unsuccessfully to escape for two consecutive nights. Finally, we were ordered to form a long line so that we could begin our journey back to the city. We would be transported, six at a time, on Chinese-made bicycles.

We were each assigned a number, and the officials began calling us in numerical order. It was about 3:00 or 4:00 p.m. and drizzling. I knew it was my last chance for escape.

If I waited in line, I was certain that I would be killed when my number, 48, was called, but if I tried to escape, there was a small chance of success.

I picked up my belongings and began running as fast as I could. The guards sprayed countless bullets at me from different directions; shooting to kill, not just as a warning.

I zigzagged and ducked flying bullets, and fell down many times.

I ran for the rest of the day and throughout the night until I finally collapsed.

Life After Death

As dawn broke, I woke to the sound of noisy footsteps, and realized I was back at the main highway. I was completely exhausted and felt numb. Motivated by fear, I got up and walked along with those who had not been placed in groups.

I met a stranger and his wife and three-year-old son. Patrick agreed to adopt me as his brother and I took on a new identity. No longer a university student or a Republican policeman, I became a laborer, a farmer, and an uneducated man.

Together we decided to leave Cambodia and search for freedom—the dream of freedom was reborn again in my mind. Thailand was our destination, but there were many obstacles. First, we didn't know how to get there; second, we didn't have any means to get there; and third, we were afraid. Patrick and I kept our dream alive by searching for a way out.

I was obsessed with the idea of leaving Cambodia, and conditioned my mind to seek freedom. I could not live under such an oppressive regime.

Plus, I was now an escapee from death row.

We eluded many check points set up by communist officials, until we reached the central provincial capital of Kampong Thom. We were captured after passing through the capital to the next town of Stuong, and were officially issued a warning not to move any further. We knew what that meant—we could be killed.

After being captured, the Khmer Rouge sent us to live in Rokar—a village in one of Cambodia's central regions, many hundreds of kilometers from Thailand's border. We were forced to work as slave laborers along with hundreds of other people.

Although we lived together, Patrick and I worked in different fields and rarely had any chance to talk to each other about our plan.

After some time had passed, the village chief's daughter appointed me to guard newly-sown rice fields from birds and animals. I was lucky, compared to others who were assigned to much more dangerous jobs. The girl tried hard to indoctrinate me.

I took the opportunity to get to know her and to win her heart and mind. By changing my mental attitude, I eventually earned her trust with kindness and compassion. I praised her for her convictions and dedication to the country and to the Khmer Rouge.

We developed mutual trust and she gradually disclosed the best ways to get to the Thai border. Every day, I used the information she provided to map out the plan in my mind.

I believe that she knew that I was planning to escape, but hesitated to advise the authority, her father, because of our friendship.

Dangrek Mountain Range...one of many obstacles between Tim and freedom.

A Plan of Escape

I managed to form a group of twelve people who wanted to escape to Thailand. It was very challenging to get everyone together to plan our journey, for we lived in different parts of the village and we were not allowed to travel without local permits.

With Patrick's encouragement, I came up with a plan and hoped that everyone would support it, which they did. After many failed attempts, one night we finally succeeded. Together, all twelve of us left the village at 1:00 a.m. I took the initiative to lead the group, as I had devised the plan. We needed to hide during the day and move only at night.

One of the most dangerous risks to our group involved Patrick's three-year-old son, who constantly cried. Sometimes, his mother had to stuff his mouth with a roll of cloth, in order for us to safely elude security guards.

From the moment we escaped, I led the group toward the jungle. I followed the directions given to me by my young Khmer Rouge friend. My plan was to avoid entering any villages; fearing communist soldiers would catch us. The rest of the group did not agree with my plan, as everyone was hungry and wanted to trade for food with the villagers.

When we reached the depths of the jungle, the group decided they did not want me to lead them anymore and they voted me out. We continued the journey under Patrick's leadership. We finally arrived on the outskirts of an unknown village, near a mountain, and Patrick decided to trade some of our clothing for potatoes and ears of corn. Everyone was happy, but I was worried and concerned. We slept in an abandoned cottage outside the village as the villagers instructed. They told us they needed to return to the village and would bring the food in the morning.

Just before daybreak, we were awakened by the sound of ox-carts, cowbells, and footsteps. A dozen communist soldiers surrounded the cottage and pointed their guns at us.

We were forced to follow them to the nearby village.

We realized that the villagers had duped us.

We were separated from each other and each of us was told that we would be brought to our final destination in the morning. Patrick told them we were on our way to join our relatives at a village near the mountain. I saw the soldiers smirk and remembered the village chief's daughter telling me that no one lived near that mountain except wild animals.

The next morning, the soldiers brought us back together. Six heavily-armed men escorted us to an unknown destination to be executed.

We all knew that it was the last day of our lives.

I tried to talk the others into an attempt to overpower the guards so we could escape. Three men out of the group agreed, but Patrick was not among them.

In the deep jungle about two kilometers away from the village, Patrick's wife became ill and fainted. We stopped, and were told by a mean-looking guard to eat our last meal for it was our last day. I asked the guard to allow us to cook a hot meal, and he agreed. We could smell a strange, foul odor from the woods nearby.

The Light of Freedom

As we were led away into the jungle, we tried to communicate amongst ourselves by using eye signals and whispers. We realized that we needed to overpower the gunmen in order to try to escape again, but only three of us decided to take this chance. While the soldiers began to relax and prepare for lunch and an afternoon nap, the two men and I dashed toward the jungle a few yards away.

Moments later, we heard a volley of gunshots as we ran.

During our difficult journey to Thailand, the three of us spoke often about our friends who were left behind, and about the chance we took in order to survive for a few more moments.

We didn't know if or when we would be re-captured or killed.

We spent long days and nights in deep jungles, inhabited by many wild animals. Sometimes we starved and other times we were dehydrated.

We stayed alive by eating wild fruit, tree leaves, and the meat of wild animals we were able to catch.

We swam across many rivers, climbed trees, hiked up countless mountains, and crossed numerous swamps and deep valleys.

We risked being killed or maimed when crossing ground laid with thousands of landmines.

I wondered whether I had done the right thing for I was unsure about my own future. However, I was determined to leave the communist regime to seek freedom—the freedom of body and mind that I had dreamed of and imagined since I was young.

I wanted to be free from hunger, fear, and oppression, and I endured much on that trip to make that dream become reality.

On August 18, 1975, approximately four months after we were forced to leave Phnom Penh, we climbed the final mountain on our dangerous journey to freedom.

At the top of that steep mountain, I felt as though I was breathing the purest air on earth. I smelled freedom and saw the dim light of liberty.

I gazed back down to our troubled land of Cambodia, thousands of meters below, and waved good-bye. I hoped that one day I would be able to bring the tastes, the sights, the sounds, and the feeling of freedom back to Cambodia.

My two friends and I joyfully hugged each other, and I quietly thanked them for giving me courage and confidence to lead our small group to safety. I felt their gratitude and appreciation in my heart.

I still remember many things that came to my mind at that pivotal moment in my life.

I thought about my small village; my parents, sisters and family; my friends; and the battles I had fought trying in vain to achieve freedom.

I thought about my uncle's family, and Sopheap, as well as Patrick and the other eight teammates who were left behind.

I cried silent tears of joy as I stepped into freedom.

Author's Note

It is estimated that one quarter of Cambodia's population (more than 2 million civilians) died during the Cambodian genocide between 1975 and 1979.[1] Over 19,000 mass graves have been discovered, often referred to as the "killing fields."[2]

Postscript

Tim and his two friends were apprehended by Thai rangers and were placed in closely-guarded confinement. Later, Tim was chosen by a local Thai official to become his family's household servant.

After spending a year as no more than an indoor slave, Tim decided to enter a Cambodian refugee camp in the Thai province of Surin, hoping for the opportunity to attain true freedom outside Thailand.

Tim continued to visualize his freedom—of body, mind, and spirit—until one day he was offered an opportunity to go to the United States, the place he had dreamed of for so many years.

Just days later, Tim met his future wife, Neang, who lived in the same refugee camp. One condition of Tim's eligibility for entry into the USA was that he travel alone. Tim decided to stay in the camp rather than leave without Neang, and they were married in the refugee camp.

His dedication and determination won the heart and soul of the late Rev. Arthur G. Pedersen of Grace Church Van Vorst, Jersey City, New Jersey. Both Tim and his wife, Neang, arrived in Jersey City in October 1976. And a new adventure began!

---

[1] World Without Genocide, William Mitchell College of Law, St. Paul, Minnesota. http://worldwithoutgenocide.org/genocides-and-conflicts/cambodian-genocide

[2] Cambodian Genocide Program, Yale University, New Haven, Connecticut. http://www.yale.edu/cgp/

Tim's emotional return to Cambodia in 2008. He is standing at the location where the Khmer Rouge soldiers transported victims to the hill (in the background) to be executed. Also, many innocent people were killed at this small mountain pond where Tim was placed on death row and escaped for the first time.

A JOURNEY THROUGH PAIN:

Tom Cunningham's Story

2

A JOURNEY THROUGH PAIN:
Tom Cunningham's Story

Childhood is typically a time of laughter, joy, and exploration. But when children face medical conditions, this season can be overshadowed by hospital visits, interventions, and pain.

My health challenges began with an early diagnosis of rheumatoid arthritis at the age of five. This condition required me to begin daily doses of pain medication, as well as the oral steroid prednisone, a medication that caused cataracts and stunted my growth, along with several other side effects.

In those early years of suffering and limitation, I heard doctors on a number of occasions tell my parents that I would likely be in a wheelchair at some point during my teenage years. I determined to do whatever it took to ensure that did not happen.

When I was 17, I was admitted to the Children's Hospital in Ottawa in order to complete a series of research tests before I was too old to meet their age criteria. This occurred during a period of time when my arthritis was not severe, and it seemed strange for my parents and sisters to visit me in hospital when I was not in dire pain or immobilized by stiffness. During that week I had two life-transforming experiences I will never forget.

My first roommate was a 13-year-old boy who was attached to several machines. Through my own limited experience, I did not understand the seriousness of his situation.

I focused on the disruptive noise his machines created, which prevented me from sleeping. During the short time we shared a room, this young boy did not receive any visitors.

After three days, he died.

It overwhelmed me to think he died alone. I was ashamed that I had only been focused on myself.

That night, alone in the room, I cried myself to sleep.

A second person who impacted me profoundly during this stay was a bedridden seven-year-old girl with cancer. I talked and joked with her a lot and also visited her while her parents were there. We would all play games together and I tried to make her laugh as much as I could.

After the boy in my room died, the girl's parents asked the nursing staff if their daughter could be moved to my room because of the relationship I had developed with her. Although I knew she was sick, I had no idea how far her cancer had progressed.

In the middle of the second night, I lost my new friend.

Having developed such a special relationship with her, I was devastated when she died.

I felt even worse for her parents. They were very kind to me, repeatedly thanking me for being so good with their daughter.

That week in the hospital made me view my painful arthritis much differently. It became crystal clear to me that there were many other young people with worse, and even fatal, diseases.

It also gave me one of the first opportunities to encourage someone else who was suffering. Befriending that girl and investing in her showed me the difference I could make in another person's life.

Today my purpose is to take every opportunity to encourage others. I credit my experience with the young girl and her parents as the first glimmer of that purpose. I believe God allowed that week to enable me to learn significant life lessons.

But my time in hospitals had only just begun.

Shortly after, I began my first year of university. This is typically an exciting time, but my physical pain became a crisis during my first semester. While friends were running from class to class, every step I took was torture.

In addition to the pain in my hip area, the joint itself was loose. It felt like it was moving in and out of my hip socket, radiating constant searing agony so intense that I felt nauseated. It took all of my mental and physical energy to endure it.

When climbing stairs, I had to hold onto the bannister as tightly as my arthritic hands, elbows, and wrists would allow. Each step was tentative in case the hip joint moved as I was putting pressure on it.

My family rallied around me to support me during this time. In order to allow me to sleep, my parents and sisters placed numerous pillows around my body.

When the least painful position was found, it was a further challenge to stay in that position long enough to fall asleep. I clearly needed a surgical intervention.

In 1981, I was introduced to an orthopedic surgeon in Ottawa named Dr. Alan Giachino. We gradually learned about each other's strengths. I benefitted from his outstanding skills and he admired my determination and courage.

At that time, hip replacement surgery was seldom considered an option. Dr. Giachino and his medical colleagues were very concerned about replacing my hip at such a young age. Since replacements were only expected to last up to 15 years, the medical team knew I would require revision surgery in my thirties.

Revision surgery is much more complicated than an original replacement because doctors have to remove the previous hardware and attach new pieces to a bone that has eroded during the previous 15 years.

Unable to bear the thought of living in my pain-ridden state, I appealed to Dr. Giachino to go ahead with the surgery. He did not want to say yes without conferring with the other orthopedic surgeons. He asked if I would agree to speak to the doctors myself at their next meeting.

I think he knew, based on our growing fondness and respect for each other, that I could convince his colleagues.

Grateful and desperate to share with those doctors my level of pain and the impact it was having on my life, I was an 18-year-old, 5-feet-1-inch force to be reckoned with.

This was a significant presentation for me.

I believed they wanted to help people be as functional as possible and I knew they had the ability to do just that, so I resolutely asked them to enhance my quality of life by operating immediately.

I painted a picture of a determined young man who desired an active, meaningful life. I was confident in my ability to cope with a revision surgery when the time came. We all trusted that future medical advances would make this surgery safer and more effective when it was needed.

I answered their questions, imagining those doctors enjoying the opportunity to help me.

Thankfully they agreed and the surgery date for my first total hip replacement was scheduled. Hope for an improved quality of life outweighed any fear I had about the surgery or recovery.

The surgery went very well, with only one complication related to my bladder. As a young person, I had never heard of a catheter, and this was the first of many times I experienced the loss of dignity that occurs with extended hospital stays.

The day after surgery, my nurse and physiotherapist tried to help me walk. To get me out of bed, they moved my body, since they knew best how to manage all the various tubes that were attached.

But once my hip felt the absence of the bed and the presence of gravity, I immediately felt a sharp, continuous pain.

They continued the motion all the way to the floor and once my leg was on solid ground, I tried to take my first step.

During recovery, I remember being surrounded by elderly people who recovered much more slowly than I did. I was grateful for this one advantage of healing that my young age provided. Hip replacement surgery caused a significant level of pain, but it was much less than I had endured before the operation.

I felt encouraged by this improvement even while I was recovering.

That hip replacement was done more than thirty years ago.

Orthopedic doctors believe this could be a world record.

Although not a record that anyone would like to have, I'll enjoy this claim to fame.

A short time after that first hip replacement, Dr. Giachino told me I would likely need my other hip replaced within a year. He used the analogy of putting a new tire on only one side of a car, and explained that the old tire would then wear out faster. In the same way, my other hip would likely wear out soon and it would also need to be replaced. He was right and my second hip replacement surgery took place just over a year later.

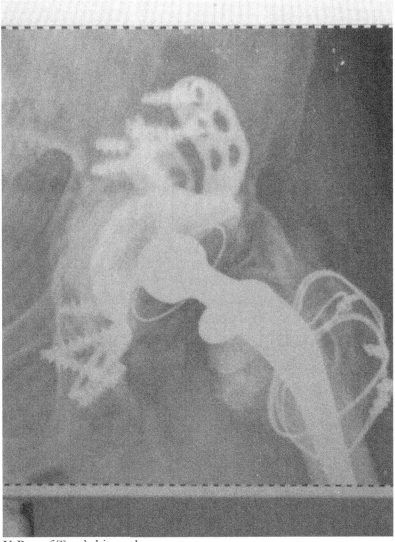

X-Ray of Tom's hip replacement

By the time I was 26, I had both hips and one knee replaced, yet my most painful surgery was yet to come. The pain I began to endure in my ankle derailed my progress and quality of life yet again. It was the beginning of the worst surgery and recovery I have ever experienced.

Rheumatoid arthritis often causes one or more joints to hurt more than the rest, and then suddenly improve. However, I came to realize ankle surgery was imminent because this next flare-up was clearly not going into remission.

I was at my lowest point ever during this season. The constant pain and disability cut me off from all activities. I was living on my own, and was practically housebound, reduced to existing rather than living. I had no idea if it was even possible to fix my ankle enough for me to ever function normally and that terrified me.

As an entrepreneur, I knew my inability to work for several months would lead to significant financial concern. This was also the first time since I was 16 that I no longer owned my own car, one more factor that triggered the start of my depression.

Out of sheer desperation, I phoned Dr. Giachino's office, begging to be seen as soon as possible.

I arrived at the hospital for my appointment and was in tears from the difficult bus ride and walk I had endured to get to the clinic. For someone who prided himself on being extremely tough, having them see me cry was embarrassing.

Dr. Giachino knew I could endure a great deal of pain and, because of my distress, he agreed to schedule the surgery immediately.

Even though I was in so much agony, I tried to remain positive. In fact, I remember him telling one of his student doctors that I was one of his most positive and resilient patients.

Because of my intense pain, I could not process the explanation of what the surgery would entail so I was not prepared for what would be my worst surgery.

The operation involved an almost total reconstruction of my right ankle to fuse it at a 90-degree angle, rather than let it fuse on its own in a less functional way. My left ankle had already fused on its own at a 45-degree angle. This means I only walk awkwardly on the balls of my left foot, which slows my pace and leads to painful calluses and corns.

Six posts were inserted through my ankle bones and shin to hold everything in place after the extensive procedure. The posts protruded two inches on each side and were attached to a frame that remained in place for four months. Not only did this look alarming, it also created a unique set of challenges.

With this contraption on my foot, I was unable to wear regular pants. Ever since the first time I was hospitalized, I did not want to dress like a patient. I refused to see visitors while wearing a hospital gown. The morning after every surgery I've had, I have always asked a nurse to help me put on a t-shirt and track pants.

My new problem was finding pants I could wear to maintain my dignity. My mom bought track pants with buttons down the side. I left the buttons at the bottom undone for easy access and it was not difficult to put them on because I didn't have to pull them up. This is just one of many interesting adaptations I have had to make while recovering from surgeries.

The physiotherapists needed to see that I could function at home before they would discharge me from my longest stay in the hospital. I could not put any weight on my ankle for six weeks after the surgery. This was not easy since my other leg had already had a hip and knee replacement. I depended on a walker more after that surgery than at any other time in my life.

I knew I was not able to live on my own to recover from this surgery. Even with home visits from nurses, physiotherapists, and personal care workers, I needed assistance around the clock. I stayed with my sister and her husband in their multi-level townhouse, and I relied on them for everything.

Every day, Lorraine or David would help me up two levels to the living room couch. From there I would host visitors, the nurse, and physiotherapist. I was often alone and felt helpless while they were away during the day. For six weeks, I spent all my waking hours on their couch. I had never had to do that after previous surgeries.

The recovery was extremely difficult for me. I am very independent and do not like requiring help from others. I also did not have a job, which meant I needed financial assistance, and I felt like a burden.

Prior to the surgery, I was self-employed. I knew I could not wait four months for the posts to be removed to begin looking for work. In a short time, I was able to secure a job interview for an accounting position at a family business. In spite of the complications of taking a handicapped bus, I was able to get to the interview on my own.

Worried because I had not mentioned my condition to the person on the phone, I felt very nervous. I could not imagine why they would hire me instead of an able-bodied person who had a vehicle.

I was relieved when I met one of the company owner's sons, who was handicapped and walked with a visible limp.

I believed God helped me obtain this job in spite of severe mobility and transportation challenges.

I faithfully went to work every day.

Although I had difficulty adjusting to being unable to drive anymore, I met many amazing individuals while taking the handicapped bus. Several faced even greater challenges than I did, yet they were happy and positive and seemed to enjoy life. Truly humbled by the people I befriended, I consider it to be one of the greatest blessings of my life to have used that bus service.

Months after surgery, I went for a follow-up appointment at Dr. Giachino's clinic.

Instead of setting a date to remove the posts from my leg, to my horror, they removed them immediately—without freezing.

I was traumatized by the whole experience and I still relive that fear and pain.

Suffering through several periods of depression, I have taken antidepressants. I have led several depression-support groups at church over the years as well. Even though I am known for my positive mental attitude, depression was something I carefully hid from people.

Probably the most depressed and dejected I have ever felt was leading up to and following my third hip replacement. My left hip had already been revised once and had an extensive collection of titanium screws along with some wires and a metal plate. All parts of the old joint and prosthesis had to be taken out and various new components installed, depending on the severity of the damage.

I had only had this second hip for four years when I started to feel a severe level of pain. The throbbing, piercing sensation was there all the time, even while sitting and sleeping. Coping with this agony was uniquely challenging since I had decided to stop taking pain medication on a daily basis.

When people asked how I was doing, I tried not to reveal the extent of my suffering. During the six weeks before I went to see a doctor, I wasn't missing any work, nor had it affected my lifestyle. Yet it was very difficult to answer "Amazing" when asked how I felt. When at my worst, I try my hardest not to let it show on my face or in my behavior. It is a challenge I set for myself to demonstrate my toughness.

I realized this pain was so severe that it would not go into remission. I finally contacted my new orthopedic surgeon, Dr. James Skipper, who by then had replaced one of my knees and one hip at Credit Valley Hospital in Mississauga.

As with all of my doctors, he and his secretary knew that I was very tough. For me to call and beg for an appointment was out of character and I was told to come immediately to the clinic.

Dr. Skipper was shocked at the x-ray results.

They revealed that two of the titanium screws in my hip had broken apart. We were both horrified and he could not believe that I was still working, let alone walking for the six weeks.

He advised that it was very dangerous for me to bear weight on that hip. The surgery to repair this dire situation had to be done at Mount Sinai Hospital, the only hospital in the area that had a bone bank.

Dr. Skipper referred me to Dr. Allan Gross, an outstanding orthopedic surgeon in the Toronto area.

Dr. Gross saw me quickly due to the severity of the problem. He immediately summoned his medical students to review my case and placed me on a "double urgent list" for surgery. The severity of the pain and the probability of a long recovery made quitting my job the only possible decision.

Dr. Gross prescribed Demerol, a very strong narcotic, for the extreme pain that was beyond my ability to manage, both mentally and physically. But Demerol made me feel nauseous.

After taking arthritis and pain medications daily from the age of five until thirty, my stomach could not handle narcotics well. They also weren't effective since they would only slightly reduce my pain. Enduring that much constant pain over a period of months wore me down and affected my thinking.

One night, around 2:00 a.m., I was so depressed and in such excruciating pain that I phoned someone, hoping that hearing another voice would distract me.

Instead of being supportive, that person asked me to call back in the morning.

I was devastated since that person knew I had never reached out like that before.

Since that time, I have made it clear to anyone I know who is suffering that they can phone me at any time, day or night.

From my experience and that of others who suffer, the most depressing hours are between midnight and 7:00 a.m. and that is when it is critical to have someone to talk to.

After a long six-week wait on the double urgent list, it was finally time to begin the surgery to fix the dislodged screws. Inside the operating room, during last-minute preparations to put me to sleep, the phone rang.

I loudly announced, "If that is for me, please tell them I'm busy for a few hours and take a message."

My comment made Dr. Gross and other staff laugh out loud. I was proud of myself for being able to remain so calm and keep my sense of humor.

The surgery was quite long, and very complicated. The following morning, Dr. Gross visited my room to give me a report. I could tell he was upset.

He apologized for nicking my sciatic nerve during the procedure and explained it would cause some permanent nerve damage. I profusely thanked him for doing such a great job with my hip. I reassured him that a little nerve damage was nothing compared to the complicated surgery he performed to put that hip together for the third time.

Dr. Gross could tell I meant it wholeheartedly since his demeanor and body language changed to relief right away.

He explained that I had required significant bone transplant and that I could not bear weight on my left leg for six to eight weeks. That meant I would need to constantly use a walker.

I was released from hospital five days after surgery, which is quite an accomplishment, considering how extensive the surgery was and how immobile I would need to be. I am very good for a surgeon's efficiency rating.

The fact that I lived alone was also a concern. I was offered the opportunity to stay at the rehabilitation hospital right next to Mount Sinai; however, I wanted to recover at home. Arrangements were made for a nurse to visit me at home daily for a few weeks; mostly for wound care, and to check for infections. A physiotherapist was also scheduled two or three days a week. Since this was my fourth hip surgery, I was familiar with the exercises I needed to do.

As always, my family was amazing. My father came to live with me for the first four days after I got home. He looked after my every need and I really enjoyed having him there.

I found it mentally challenging to be so limited in what I could do; even getting in and out of my chair required help. My mother lived close by and she and my dad were both tremendous blessings before and after the surgery.

This was my first surgery since I began attending Heartland, A Church Connected. I had established many great friendships there. During my time in the hospital, and while recovering at home, the outpouring of love and support I received from Pastor Gary Stagg and my friends from church was overwhelming. I had many people visit me in hospital and the visits continued when I got home.

My freezer was filled with homemade food.

I cannot put into words how much that love and support meant to me during my recovery.

After my father returned home, navigating my apartment was frustrating, exhausting, and time consuming. Simple routines took much longer than usual.

To get to the bathroom, I had to hop on one foot while using my walker. Once there, numerous moves and contortions were required to position the walker out of the way so I could stand by the sink.

Getting dressed also took much longer than my already time-consuming process. Since I have not been able to bend down for many years, I have used a dressing stick to pull my pants up.

At this point, I had to use the stick to put the pants on without putting weight on my left leg. I was also not allowed to get the wound wet while it was healing, which meant I could not shower for several weeks. As a result, I had to wash myself while standing on one foot at the bathroom sink and navigating around the walker.

The extra time and energy required to do simple, daily activities was very tough on me mentally as well as physically. Tasks like getting up from my chair to get a drink or food were much more difficult, and I would often wait until my next visitor arrived.

I spent the majority of my time sitting in my recliner watching television or reading. I knew I needed to rest after such extensive surgery, but found this extremely difficult and depressing. I am an active person with many friends and I love to be engaged in the outside world. Although visitors helped my boredom, the effort to socialize was also exhausting.

During this time of recovery, I had a unique opportunity that launched the next stage of my life. I was asked to speak at a Christmas lunch for a financial company. My mother drove me to and from the event and helped me enter the building.

I walked to the stage and spoke while steadying myself with my walker. It was a surreal experience for me to speak to a group of about 100 people.

I shared a message entitled "No Excuses," using my walker to illustrate how easy it would have been for me to make excuses. I was proud of this presentation and for the positive impact on the audience.

This speaking opportunity was a welcome highlight during this discouraging season. The audience's reaction made me realize my message could encourage and inspire others. That alone seemed to dispel the depression of the previous three months and it motivated me to stay strong and positive.

This change propelled me to start a new home-based business that benefited charity and generated leads for the financial company that hired me to speak.

With renewed purpose and an endeavor that aligned with my skills, I soon regained my usual optimistic outlook.

Tom's journey gets 20,000+ website visits per month from over 50 countries

LESSONS LEARNED

Throughout my journey, I have learned important life lessons. I hope these will benefit others as they have impacted me.

Plan Positively—Before Challenges Come

I read at least one non-fiction book every week to learn from people who contribute positively to the world. In spite of the tremendous challenges that many of these authors have endured, they refuse to allow obstacles to limit them.

Many of these books leave me thinking, "If they can flourish with their challenges, then I can definitely flourish with mine."

By filling my mind with positive messages, I can recognize when my thoughts drift toward being negative and begin to change my mindset. Once I recognize my "stinking thinking," I redirect my thoughts to either applicable Bible verses, or to people I know or have read about who succeed through much worse situations than I will ever face.

It is hard for me to keep thinking about my constant aches when I read about Nick Vujicic or Kyle Maynard, who were born without arms or legs.

When I get upset about dropping something and not being able to pick it up, I remember that 40 percent of the world lives on less than two dollars per day and that they would gladly trade places with me. Without this discipline of intentionally focusing on positive material, many people are unprepared for inevitable challenges. They lack positive examples to draw strength from.

The key is to think or act positively in advance of challenges because it is almost impossible to develop mental clarity and resiliency in the midst of a crisis.

Value Role Models

I try to find role models who maintain a positive attitude and take constructive action while contending with difficulties. Hosting a radio show enables me to interview everyday heroes.

I spend an hour drawing out their wisdom about facing their various challenges. Filling my thoughts with the stories of these inspirational heroes gives me perspective about my pain and disability.

One such hero is my friend Mike. I used to drive Mike to dialysis once or twice a week. Despite my pain tolerance, I have an embarrassing weakness related to needles and veins. I can hardly endure an intravenous needle, and even talking about veins makes me feel ill. Dialysis patients know all about needles because they have to regularly be hooked up to a machine that filters and cleans their blood.

Mike told me how much he admired me for living with as much pain as I endure. I told Mike how much I admired him for living with kidney problems and enduring dialysis.

Even though our illnesses were different, those discussions helped solidify my personal contentment. Although living with rheumatoid arthritis is very difficult, I choose to be content that I do not have to face other unique challenges where I might not be able to cope as well.

Embrace Creativity

My physical limitations have helped me learn to be creative. Because almost every joint in my body has range of motion restrictions, or complete fusions, I have to do many everyday tasks differently. One main challenge is picking things up off the ground.

When I can, it involves creativity. When I cannot, I need my reacher or someone else to do it for me. One way I pick things up is to put them between my feet, sit down, then throw the object in the air with my feet and legs and catch it on the way down.

I also use a dressing stick to pick up my underwear and socks and to pull up my pants.

Since I am 5 foot 1 inch, many items are not accessible to me. I use some very creative methods to reach things on shelves, and catch them on the way down. Using the skills, talents, and abilities needed to endure your challenge provides purpose and direction. Focusing on the things you can do provides hope; this includes finding new and creative ways to overcome obstacles.

Pay Attention to Words

Words are powerful—both spoken and unspoken. It is natural for even the most positive person to think negatively at times. Our inner thoughts can plant powerful negative messages in our minds, leading to discouragement.

Once you verbalize those negative thoughts, especially in the presence of other people, you are also releasing negative energy into their lives. Being careless and lazy about the words we choose to express our thoughts and feelings hurts not only ourselves but also the people around us.

Friends and family know that I am in pain all the time. I tend not to talk about it, unless directly asked, and they do not usually ask me how my pain is. This allows for a more positive energy in our interactions.

Encouraging others to live positively through the challenges of life is a priority for me; therefore, I prefer not to verbalize any negative thoughts about my constant pain.

Pay close attention to the words you speak and those that are simply formed thoughts—knowing their impact is great.

Seek Contentment, Not Happiness

Pursuing happiness is the topic of many books and corporate slogans. Unfortunately, pursuing happiness as a goal will often lead to decisions and actions that weaken character, integrity, and reputation. In contrast, seeking contentment will help you more effectively process the challenges and tough times. Focusing your thoughts on contentment forces you to examine the positive aspects of your situation.

People who have been married a long time often learn this lesson or use this principle and it is one of the keys to a strong relationship. Every husband and wife does things that occasionally annoys the other spouse. People who stay married keep in mind all the positive traits that they love in their spouse, and that helps them live with the few annoying habits their spouse displays.

They are content with the many things they love about the person they married and this helps diffuse the few quirks in their character. Gary Thomas supports this idea in his book, *Sacred Marriage*, when he writes,

"What if God designed marriage to make us holy, rather than to make us happy?"

Our own natural goals to be happy are misguided and it is important to pursue more lasting emotions such as contentment.

Challenge the "Deserve Better" Thinking

If you continually think "why me?" and are convinced you deserve better, you will never develop the attitude of gratitude necessary to endure suffering well. Why would we assume we deserve more than someone else?

Illness is no respecter of persons. Disease and tragedy strike regardless of gender, social status, or ethnicity.

The flip side is that we do not always value the many blessings that we already have. Even living in a developed country is a global blessing that gives us advantages we do not deserve any more than a person living in a third world country on less than two dollars per day deserves to live there.

I tell audiences that 70 percent of people who get rheumatoid arthritis are women so I could ask,

"Why me, Lord? Why not my sister Lorraine?"

Asking "Why me?" is dangerous. Enduring difficult things we did nothing to cause can be mentally and physically draining.

It is an act of futility that can lead us further down the path toward self-pity and despair. It is far more effective to shift from "Why me?" to "How can I be my best despite this situation?"

I focus on using adversity to help myself and others. I know first-hand how very difficult adversity and challenges are. Living with pain throughout my body, together with restrictions in all of my joints for the past 45 years, means that I have many times questioned my adversity, and even my desire for a long life.

Yet millions of people face unbelievably difficult circumstances.

Deliberately forcing ourselves to ask how suffering can serve a purpose is not easy. There are moments when we despair and feel alone in our pain. Yet pushing through these emotions is a challenging, but worthwhile process.

Rheumatoid arthritis is my lifelong reality but I refuse to allow it to define the quality of my relationships and experiences.

Where some might see problems, I see possibilities.

Where others might see obstacles, I see opportunities.

I set my goals high and refuse to allow my physical limitations to stand in my way.

I strive to process my pain in productive ways and share a message of hope with anyone facing challenges.

Tom speaking at the Napoleon Hill International Convention in March 2012

A JOURNEY PAST
DEFEAT
AND
FEAR:

Taylor Tagg's Story

ADVERSITY TO ADVANTAGE

3

A JOURNEY PAST DEFEAT AND FEAR:
Taylor Tagg's Story

Defeat is the greatest teacher of them all.

Until my early forties, I struggled to work through the mental and emotional fallout of childhood abuse, which I chronicled in the book *The Path to a Peaceful Heart.*

In the depths of that thirty-year struggle, I discovered I could walk through my fears and assign new meaning not only to my good experiences, but to the bad ones as well. Defeat did not have to remain something that got me down.

Defeat did indeed rule my life for a long time, until I realized that it could become my most powerful instructor and my guru, if I allowed it to be.

I want to give you my perspective on two of the biggest defeats I have ever gone through.

The lessons that came from these two experiences changed my thinking forever, and impacted the way I now perceive everything that comes in and out of my life.

Yes, defeat is your greatest teacher if you choose to learn from it.

My course in defeat was never more apparent than the massive mistake I made while working for a transportation company.

It was a busy time of year. We were at the end of the winter quarter when all the accounting data had to be neatly categorized and presented for company investors. One of my responsibilities was to move dollars from one accounting "bucket" to another to satisfy the industry reporting rules.

Although this process was not something that was done on a regular basis, I considered myself competent at this type of role, and the team was comfortable with me handling the task.

It was so busy, and extremely chaotic, with all of the team rushing to meet our multiple deadlines, in addition to having only two days left to finish the final investors' copy. We stayed up late for five nights in a row, checking and double-checking our facts and figures, before the final paperwork was due.

Although I was exhausted, I was confident I had accurately verified my portion of the accounting data. I remember saying to a co-worker,

"Well, I wonder what the final numbers will look like this time," anticipating another positive benchmark toward our year-end company performance bonus.

It became a routine: brew another Royal Cup Bold pot of coffee, cream, two sweeteners, and ensure the checklist was cleared of all duties before I signed off on another great quarter.

I remember the feeling of relief at being finished and celebrating with the team, who had worked hard to get to the finish line; now we could finally relax and take a much-deserved break.

Suddenly a thought hit me like a bolt of lightning from the clear blue sky.

"Oh No! I forgot to reclassify the debt."

At the most critical time of this financial reporting phase, I had made a massive mistake!

I had failed to move the borrowed capital dollars from one accounting "bucket" to another to comply with accounting rules.

This particular transaction wasn't something that was done regularly. As a matter of fact, it happened only once every couple of years.

Well, I didn't get it done. Every two years or not, it had slipped by me.

This wouldn't be a big deal if the amount was a few dollars, but it was $200 million dollars!

I panicked.

My chest seized up in knots as I realized my mistake was possibly too late to fix. All the reporting information was being submitted to the financial consolidators so they could prepare the final report.

My mouth suddenly tasted like gunmetal. For a moment, I thought I was going to throw up.

"What is going to happen?" I thought. "It's $200 million dollars!"

My first rational thought after the information sank into my mind was one of terror. "Will I have a job next week? I've made a serious error! Oh wow Taylor, how could you forget this?"

Just a few minutes before, I had been so proud of "getting it all right" and of what the team had accomplished, only to have those thoughts shattered by the news that my lack of attention was going to make the team look incompetent and disorganized to upper management.

That thought devastated me.

I thought to myself, "What did I do to deserve this? How did I not see this coming?"

Like a quarterback getting pummeled by a weakside blitz, I felt totally blindsided and confused.

I got my bearings again, dusted myself off, and tried to make sense of what had just happened.

"What did I do?" I thought.

Then the anger arrived. I could feel the warm blood coursing through my bulging veins. I clenched my teeth almost to the point of cracking a lower one. How could I have let this pass me by?

My mind began to simultaneously process and deal with the mental and physical symptoms of disappointment and anger.

"Calm down," I told myself. "First things first. Let management know. Get this thing fixed somehow. NOW!!"

With my head hanging low, I walked into the manager's office to let him know what had happened.

Immediately, all hell broke loose. Something had to be done quickly or this would be a terribly timed misidentification of the company's liabilities. The phone lines started buzzing with hurried chatter and rushed action. The air felt very thick and hot. I stood in my manager's office as the room began to swirl and sway and cave in around me

It seemed like hours of torture, but likely only took several minutes to assess if, in fact, an adjustment to the numbers could be made at such a late point in the reporting process.

"If we don't get to change this, I'm cooked! My career is over!"

I thought about all the overtime and late nights I had put into this job, all of the experience I had gained, and all the good things I contributed to the team. In that moment, it seemed as though it all meant nothing . . . Poof! Gone!

Finally, after breathless anticipation, we got the clearance to move the $200 million to its correct place.

I almost fainted on the floor. As sweat dripped down my back, I gave a huge sigh of relief that all the numbers would be okay, and then I sank down into the big red office chair and exclaimed, "Whew!"

In the aftermath of my mistake, the financial statements had to be republished internally because of the oversight. That's a big no-no for accountants. Companies don't want to readjust anything that might conceivably give the appearance of incorrect numbers, even though all of the figures were indeed accurate.

Many of the top executives in the company were briefed on the situation. This wasn't a "look the other way" scenario.

Someone had to pay, and that someone was me.

This was a large internal mistake and unfortunately it was going to cost me something.

Could I feel any worse?

No.

My stomach was in knots for days.

This crisis seemed to come out of nowhere. I have played a lot of sports in my life and had some pretty tough and heartbreaking losses, but this particular defeat was one of the hardest to deal with because it was all my fault.

In a flash my reputation was damaged, I let my team down, and made the organization look bad; all because I didn't perform my job correctly. Even worse, the checks and balances of my team failed as well. Both a co-worker and the manager missed the check on the reclassification dates.

Several times, the thought of making excuses to shift the blame away from me sounded like a brilliant idea.

I could have said, "Uh, the system is flawed. My co-workers and manager missed it too. I mean no one was looking for it."

I realized quickly that this was the cowardly way out. In the thick of assessing responsibility for this mess, my name and reputation was going to suffer.

Several times, a little voice inside kept saying,

"Do the right thing, Taylor."

Laying blame would have been a short-term way to feel better about the situation, but unfortunately, there was no feeling good about that option at all. If I accepted full responsibility for everything up front, my career would suffer in the short term, but eventually all would fade away, and the freedom to move forward in the company would resume at some point.

If blame shifted away from me right away, then others on the team would suffer greatly in the short term and I would be free, but would it ever really feel like freedom?

No.

Who was I kidding?

Guilt would set in for the long haul and I would be shunned by my team. Truth be told, standing up and admitting that the oversight was mine was truly the correct action to take. At the end of the day, I messed up and it hurt.

It wasn't a tough decision. It was the right one.

I accepted my mistake and owned it 100 percent.

And that's when the lessons from this horror story began to filter into my mind.

What was I learning from all of this? I was learning that defeat could be my greatest teacher if I was open to that possibility.

But it stung badly.

The lack of attention to an important but irregular accounting task was solely on my shoulders. Several investigative meetings followed as to why the error happened.

Written reprimands came my way.

The odds of coming out of this thing with my job intact looked rather dim.

Upon meeting with management to go over the situation, an unexpected situation presented itself. The worst defeat of my financial career became a great opportunity, affirming the belief that there is a redemptive side to every adverse situation.

Management had the patience and understanding to ask me to create a new process of improvement for the team, one that ensured mistakes like this would never happen again.

Not everyone gets a chance to make a wrong into a right.

You create it.

Both management and I were willing to find the good in a really tough mistake.

That was a blessing in disguise.

I submitted a proposal to hold a new quarterly meeting to address items and issues that were not part of the normal accounting routine. That way, irregular accounting tasks could be brought to the team's attention long before the end of the reporting cycle and long before it was too late to do anything about it.

Management gladly accepted my proposal. This enabled me to put the finishing touches on turning a very difficult defeat into something positive for others.

My lack of action was a lesson in awareness for the team's future. A golden opportunity that arose from the jaws of career defeat has since saved many other co-workers from making key and important errors like mine. Today, that quarterly meeting still has important significance at the company.

Had I not accepted the responsibility of the mistake up front, the chance to correct the error would never have been complete. Guilt would have swallowed me from the inside out, with no positive outcomes ever having a chance to rise to the surface.

By allowing this mistake to teach me how to lead and how to step up even when I had failed miserably, I gained the courage to embrace freedom and turn a heartbreaking obstacle into opportunity.

By accepting my part 100 percent, I was able to work to make the situation better for others.

I found and applied the good that came from the error.

Opportunities exist in every single mistake.

Any adversity or defeat can be viewed as something positive if you decide to change your perspective on whether it helps you grow or continues to haunt you.

Feelings of guilt and anger can be converted into positive feelings of serving others through mistakes. Exercise positive choice. Doing this can change your life forever. It did for me.

Defeat can become your greatest teacher if only you will allow it to show you the path to victory.

Trust in that.

One Word That Transformed How I View Every Life Experience

Significant life change can happen with just the smallest shift in perspective. This happened to me when I shifted one single word in my vocabulary—just one word made all the difference in the world!

I replaced the word *To* with the word *For.*

Let me explain.

When I was younger, my objectives were to avoid pain and to feel good.

Isn't that what we all try to do?

Anything that got in the way of feeling good was detrimental to my objective in life. Life was about goodness and enjoyment and I cursed anything that got in the way of that! As a young man, I experienced a number of abusive circumstances within a short period of time that were hard to dodge or avoid.

The feeling registered within my mind and body that these things were happening *to* me.

Have you ever felt that way?

If things didn't go according to plan, I thought it was God's way of punishing me for not being good enough. Life itself was keeping me from going forward.

If you can identify, let's count some of the ways we validate that feeling of life happening *to* us. We make excuses, and blame it on something or someone else, because accepting responsibility for our actions or words hurts too much. We hear and say these power-robbing phrases:

"He won't let me . . ."
"I can't do it because . . ."
"If only she would change . . ."
"It's all his fault because . . ."
"It's holding me back . . ."
"I don't have enough time . . ."
"Life sucks . . ."
"It won't work now because it never has before . . ."

Being a victim of life is a powerless thought process that causes endless suffering. I, too, experienced that way of thinking. It's a terrible price that we pay over and over, and one that keeps our own successes and desires at arm's length.

Not taking responsibility for one's own actions and periods of self-pity keep a person locked up in a prison of their own making—that is until he or she decides that freedom must become more important than suffering.

Often, the very thing you complain about to other people and blame others for is the perfect unfolding of what needs to be addressed in yourself.

If you make excuses often and look for others to fix your problems, then unfortunately, you are giving your power away.

Feelings and thoughts are first experienced internally before you begin seeing those traits in everyone else. Blaming is a natural defense mechanism that keeps us from becoming all we are meant to be. Blaming serves a purpose.

It ensures that we don't have to feel anything because when we feel, it hurts too much. We cope by transferring thoughts and feelings onto someone else.

Shifting blame causes negative reactions from other people and creates even more blaming from all sides. However, your life doesn't have to be that way.

You can choose otherwise.

Do you want to know how to go from victim to victor?

Take your power back by taking 100 percent responsibility for your thoughts and feelings. How do you do this?

Begin by changing *to me* into *for me*.

Life is not happening *to me*, life is happening *for me*!

What does *for me* mean? *For me* means that everything I experience has value and purpose in life. Everything that has happened, both good and bad, has taken place to teach me exactly what I can't learn any other way.

Every word, every heartbreak, every defeat, every good thing that has taken place is meant for me, so I may expand, grow, and be a better person because I choose it.

Allow this mindset change to sink into your heart and mind and you will be greatly rewarded with opportunities to unleash your potential, rather than continuing to make even more excuses to keep yourself small and hidden.

Why did the $200 million mistake have to happen *to* me?

It didn't.

That mistake happened *for* me so I could expand into accepting 100 percent responsibility instead of 85 percent or 50 percent.

It happened *for* me so I could think of my team instead of myself.

It happened *for* me so I could plug a gap in our accounting process, enabling occasionally-occurring items to be noticed and adjusted well before it was too late to do anything about them.

When life begins happening *for* you, you can take a significant step to assign different meaning and purpose to the circumstances.

Instead of a situation that could have ended my financial career, it became a circumstance that helped improve the accounting department's timeliness in reporting information. Had I not looked for the equivalent benefit in my mistake, the opportunity to improve would never have come about.

Changing one tiny word in your vocabulary—*to* into *for*—makes the impossible possible.

This new meaning now empowers me instead of decimating me.

Change one word . . . change your life. Amazing!

The Defeat of Paralyzing Fear

Speaking in front of a room full of people used to be mortifying.

The slightest possibility of making a mistake and looking like a complete moron froze every tendon and muscle in my body to the point that lying in a coffin seemed to be a better option than speaking in public.

Being verbally and mentally berated as a child did a masterful job of instilling fear in me; fear of using my voice, fear of speaking up, fear of standing up for myself, and fear that I was not good enough to be listened to.

So naturally, the thought of speaking and failing made me double over in physical pain.

Public speaking was at the top of my list of "things to avoid." After writing my first book, *Enrich Your Sunrise*, in 2003, the thought of speaking in front of groups about the book seemed like an achievable feat, but that little voice in my head saying "are you crazy?" kept making an appearance.

At 32 years of age, I decided my book was something people needed to know about. In order to tell the world about my book, something drastic had to happen to overcome my fear of public speaking.

What could I do?

I found a local Toastmasters group (a nonprofit educational organization operating clubs worldwide for the purpose of helping members improve their communication, public speaking, and leadership skills), and checked out what most said was a safe and positive environment to overcome the fear of speaking.

In that first Toastmasters meeting, the group asked me to stand and talk about myself for one minute.

I froze like an icicle.

In that moment, the thought of running out of the room and back into the safety of my comfort zone felt like a rational plan to me.

Although I didn't run, speaking wasn't going to be on the agenda either.

So, I politely passed.

No one said a thing, but inside the embarrassment was weakening my knees. I had come to a speaking club to look fear in the face and quash my inhibitions and, when it was my opportunity to speak, I passed! Ahhhhh!

My head stayed buried in my hands for several seconds.

Unexpectedly, a solution came out of my mouth.

"I'll come back next week and do it," I said. "Hmmmmm . . . did I really just say that?" I wondered. The audience graciously accepted my offer.

During the following week, I rehearsed my one-minute speech until I began to feel confident.

A little pep talk ensued, "You can do this Taylor. No, you *will* do this."

However, as I entered the Toastmasters class the following week, my heart beat faster as fear took over, gripping my body like a heavyweight boxer's headlock. Thoughts of embarrassment and defeat seemed to envelop my entire person.

I thought, "Why did I sign up for this torture again?"

Finally, my name was called. "Taylor, are you ready?"

Dripping with sweat, I got up only to find my legs felt like concrete posts. Once again, running away felt like a great option, but seriously, how fast could these cement-block legs move?

I managed to take a deep breath. Exhale!

"I will do this. I have to find the courage to do it," I thought.

I gathered myself and took another deep breath.

I sent up a prayer, a Hail Mary so to speak. "Mother of God, I need you now more than any time in my life."

As I got to the podium and started to speak, the words fumbled out.

"Please! Help me!" I thought. "Is this one minute over yet? Does someone have a dry towel for my face?" Only a few seconds had passed.

Time felt like molasses dripping from a jar; slow and slower. I amateurishly continued. The end of that one minute couldn't come fast enough.

But remarkably, something happened midway through the minute that changed my belief in my speaking ability forever.

In the middle of describing myself, the nerves quieted. I realized some of the audience actually seemed interested in what I was saying. This was a departure from when I first got to the podium; I was focused on me and what I needed to say.

As I began to talk, I focused on the audience. I realized they didn't want to tear me down like I thought they would.

They wanted to hear what I had to say.

I began to speak clearly and started to excel. People began paying even more attention to my words.

Suddenly I thought, "This isn't as bad as you thought it was going to be, is it Taylor?"

No!

The next thing I knew, complete sentences were flowing out of my mouth. As if someone had flipped a switch, a humble spark of confidence surged throughout my body.

"I can do this," I told myself.

In that instant, I had an epiphany: my deathly fear of public speaking was the only thing holding me back.

And I had just stepped through it.

It was as if I had been walking through a dense fog all my life until I suddenly saw the light burning the fog away midway through the speech. I knew I was going to finish the minute strong. The thought even arose to keep going! My confidence grew exponentially stronger second by second.

"Yes, I can do this! I am doing this! Oh my goodness, I did it!"

The audience clapped for me.

As I walked away from the front of the room, peeling back the soaked white button-down shirt stuck to my chest, I knew I was a different man than the one who had limped up to the podium just a minute earlier.

"Yes! I CAN speak! And they want to hear more!"

I knew there was a long, long way to go to develop my speaking ability, but my belief about what I was capable of totally changed within one single minute.

As I sat back in my chair with the rest of the audience, thoughts of what the fear of speaking had cost me surfaced quickly.

"You are staying small and hidden, Taylor. It's time to grow as a speaker."

Thoughts rushed to my mind of all the times I *wanted* to speak, but something told me, "No, you can't do that!"

As a little boy, I dreamed of being a speaker who influenced people in a positive way. For the longest time, I knew I wanted to help people overcome their problems and grow. It was like breath to me. Essential.

I would watch Tony Robbins deliver marvelous and influential speeches that moved people to immediate action. I saw my uncle, Father Joseph L. Tagg III, touch many people's hearts at Sunday Mass with his powerful messages of faith and forgiveness. I listened to tapes of Dr. Napoleon Hill motivating his audiences into great action and positive thought patterns.

Why couldn't I be one of those people?

What was keeping me from doing that, from living my dreams?

It took willingness and the guts to say, "*I will*, whatever it takes"; a willingness to step through the fear and keep on going even though it was likely that many setbacks and obstacles would arise.

Face your defeats and fears by embracing courage. Do whatever your heart desires. Live your dreams. Overcome whatever is before you. It just takes enough gusto, together with a little know-how, to step through your fear; even the big fears that paralyze you.

Once you step through the fear, you will see it was just a false belief that you bought hook, line, and sinker.

That's not your fault. The important thing is not that you bought into the old, false belief, but that you found the fortitude to give it up and create a new one that works.

Fear is an illusion of the mind.

Instead of avoiding your fear, allow it to come in and take a seat. Then stand up and step into and through your fear. To get through it, you must be willing to allow the fear to come true.

More than 90 percent of the time, it won't. But if it does, think through what you would do to get through that situation and survive. Then, allow yourself to let the fear go.

Unwillingness to face the fear keeps it alive and well and allows it to grow.

Facing your fear stops it in its tracks and instantly charts a new course for growth.

How long will you allow fear to run your life? Does fear really deserve space in your head? Until that fear comes true, commit to giving it absolutely no free-rent space in your mind.

Be very confident that if your fear does somehow come true, you will still be okay.

Things will work out in the end.

Trust in yourself.

You will live to tell about it.

Taylor at one of his first speaking engagements in Jackson, MS in 2003.

Whatever You Focus On, You Get More Of

If you want to transform your defeats into lessons, you need to follow up those lessons with positive action. You do this simply by *finding the good* in each person and situation in your life.

When you accept that any defeat can be overcome and triumphed over with positive action, life comes full circle. Nothing ever happens negatively without its positive equivalent present. It's a matter of deciding to focus on something different to transcend the defeat.

If you only focus on what went wrong, you will get a lot more of what went wrong.

So, how do you make defeat work for you every time?

Find the Good: Be Grateful For What You Have Right Now

A lesson is just a lesson until it is applied and accepted within your mind and heart.

The "act" of finding the good in the defeat, person, or situation is the evidence that learning has begun. When you find the good, you operate in a greater energy than where your defeat occurred.

Find anything positive. Any good will do. What are you grateful for in your life in this moment?

Maybe it's the clothes the person was wearing, a nice gesture they made, or the fact that he or she was helpful in a previous situation. Find something good, even if it is an infinitely small thing. Finding the good leads to the experience of love.

The experience of love opens us all to endless possibilities and solutions. The more one operates in a state of love, the more he or she sees all the options in common everyday challenges.

Also, people naturally want to be around those who operate in a loving way.

In a business sense, we love everyday with *service* to our team, our customers, our company, and ourselves.

As you look at life to find more of the good, realize that kindness and love are most effective when they originate *from* you. Loving yourself is the key to becoming kinder and more loving. If you can love yourself, you can love others exponentially more.

You cannot give to another what you do not possess in yourself. Cultivate kindness and love. Finding it in yourself first gives your mind's eye and heart the ability to *see* it in everyone else.

Allow kindness and love to begin with you.

Why isn't this easier to do?

The intense critic in us plays a big part in holding us back from what we want. The lasting legacy I want to leave behind is one of kindness, love, and forgiveness. The critic in me was killing that legacy, so it had to go.

Kindness and love are much more effective than criticism and blame. The former lifts while the latter deflates.

Over time, the observer in me became aware of how critical my thoughts were. My solution was to be kinder by "catching" myself doing good, like complimenting someone or encouraging them to keep going. I also began my day by verbalizing five things I was grateful for. These small acts are game changers.

Reinforce that which you want to build on. Like my mother-in-law used to say to my wife as she was growing up, "Brush your teeth, but only the ones you want to keep."

I cherish Napoleon Hill's application of the Golden Rule. It's a game changer in allowing defeat to help you. Here is a paraphrased version of the Golden Rule:

"What you do to or for another person, you do to or for yourself."

You have already begun a life-affirming change in your life by simply changing *to* into *for*, which automatically moves you from a state of blame to a state of courage, from powerlessness into power. Continue to move on by finding the good in everything and everyone.

You don't need a lesson in how to find the good in a person or situation. You already know how. You just need to know that you have the ability to rise above your circumstance in any given moment.

It's a choice.

Focus on the good. Practice gratitude.

You have all the necessary tools to overcome. You have all power within you.

Own it.

Exercises: The Four Questions in Overcoming Adversity and Defeat

As an Emotional Intelligence Expert, Forgiveness Educator, and Strategic Intervention Coach, there are four questions I ask my clients to help them work through adversity and defeat with kindness and love.

These questions and exercises are meant to assist you in cultivating belief in yourself, seeing a brighter reality, and changing your perspective from negative to positive, while taking action in response to your answers.

Approach each question with complete openness and acceptance of the answers you get. Some of the answers may surprise you. That's fine.

The heart and the mind will provide new ways of dealing with difficulty in your life and that might be scary. Go with it anyway.

God, Infinite Divinity, the Universe, or whatever Higher Power you believe in, will help you overcome the adversity and defeat if you will surrender to the path and allow it to work on your behalf.

Here are the Four Questions:

1. Is this adversity temporary?

2. What is this adversity currently costing me and how long am I willing to pay that price?

3. What is this adversity teaching me?

4. How do I apply this teaching?

   Extra: What is the positive replacement for the negative energy that I feel?

Question 1: Is This Adversity Temporary?

Question 1 sounds easy and so simple, but is it really?

Do you really believe that in time you will overcome your defeat, or are you still wrestling with the fact that you might never get the answers you need? By asking question one, you have just introduced the possibility that your problem might indeed have an end date.

Simply put, you can overcome your difficulty if you decide that is what you are going to do. You don't need the answers to already be there.

You just need to decide it is time to change. Once you decide, the answers will appear, and the next step will become apparent.

Is it time to see your difficulty as temporary?

Once you fully commit to something, you open your mind to the part of the brain that can bring you the answer.

Have you ever had the feeling that things were falling into place and you didn't have to do anything?

This is what happens when you decide with definiteness of purpose that you will do something. Thoughts begin to align.

One of my favorite authors is Norman Vincent Peale, who wrote the famous book, *The Power of Positive Thinking*.

In his book, *The Tough-Minded Optimist*, Peale relates the story of his fifth grade teacher, who would write the word CAN'T on the blackboard in large letters and then ask the students what to do. As they chanted "Strike the T off the CAN'T," he'd erase the letter, turning it into CAN.

He'd then tell the class a phrase that young Norman never forgot, "You can if you think you can."

Talk about changing a word to change your life; let's just change a single letter.

Say it. "*I Can.*"

Yes, you can.

Dr. Peale's teacher was correct. To shift your perspective from *I Can't* to *I Can* produces miraculous results. You can go from negative to positive in an instant and change your thinking from detrimental to beneficial in less than a second. But that shift doesn't happen unless you really believe in it.

Let's expand the box on Dr. Peale's thoughts one step further. Change *I Can* to *I Will*.

Say it. "*I Will.*"

Use of *I Will* is definitive, purposeful, and exact. *I Can* is solid positive thinking and it indicates that action might or might not be taken. *I Can* means I'm capable and I believe, but I may or may not act on it. An *I Will* statement guarantees that action is imminent.

I Will opens the mind to solutions. *I Will* invokes intention. Intention is acted upon by whatever means are available to the mind.

Your *will* is the most powerful tool in your personal toolbox. Your will is your method to activate faith and belief in yourself and define exactly what you plan to accomplish, although, in the end, the result may look much different than the original vision.

Never mind that.

You will not get to the end result unless you invoke your will to establish an intention and set positive action in motion.

My will was instrumental in pushing me to get in front of the Toastmasters audience and step through my fear of public speaking. Even after everything in my body and mind said no, my will and my purpose said yes. Your will gives you strength in times of weakness and courage in times of fear.

Invoke your will!

Now, let's develop some *I Will* statements for your life. Tell yourself what you *will* do right now and then begin doing it with immediate action!

I WILL _____.

I WILL _____.

I WILL _____.

I WILL _____.

I WILL _____.

Question 2: What is This Adversity Costing Me?

Often, significant life change happens with just the smallest shift in perspective. That happened to me when I changed one single word in my vocabulary—just one word made all the difference in the world! I changed *To* into *For*.

The key to question 2 is to first identify what your situation is costing you.

What is it doing to you?

How is it holding you back?

What is it keeping you from accomplishing in your life?

How long are you willing to pay that cost?

Write down on paper what that person or situation is doing to you. You might be surprised while doing this exercise. Give it a chance. List it all. Write about what kind of person he or she has been in your life. Let the truth out of the bag.

Write about what you wished for so desperately in your life, but that situation has kept you from having. Write it all down. Get it out of you now.

Allow any emotions around that situation or person to surface and let the emotions go.

For example, "My boss has kept me from advancing in this company. He is a jerk and he only looks out for himself. He has cost me a promotion and a raise!"

Write it out or speak it aloud in private.

The first key to overcoming anything is identifying it. Once you have identified what your adversity is and, more importantly, what the tangible costs are, it becomes real. Feel that cost for a moment. Let it in.

Just like I let the $200 million dollar financial mistake keep me up at night, I let it in. Then let it out and let it go. I used it to grow. Processing the negative creates the opportunity to bring about positive solutions.

Once you have listed the costs of your adversity, you will be happy to learn that nothing that has ever happened to you was in vain.

Everything has a purpose. Everything has a place.

Good, bad, right, wrong, up, and down; all of life has value.

A situation that seems to be a waste of time or that has caused you undue suffering has meaning if you will decide and choose to see it as such. When you allow yourself to honestly count the costs of your pain and suffering, you are ready to answer question 3.

Question 3: What is This Adversity Teaching Me?

Trust in what is possible. Life is always teaching us and presents us with opportunities to learn the very thing our soul needs to know.

Adversity and defeat will happen. We can't avoid them. Tough situations are an inevitable part of our journey. Those situations help us learn how to overcome pain and suffering and use those tragedies as a means to grow and prosper and help others do the same.

This is the meaning you can assign to your trials and tribulations in order to allow you to realize your highest fulfillment.

Adversity and defeat can become powerful to you because you have the ability to transform a personal liability into an asset by asking for and accepting the lessons these experiences taught you.

You were placed in your difficulty to learn the lessons of your lifetime.

What are the lessons your adversity and defeat are teaching you?

This is such an important question to answer.

The answers you provide can literally change your life forever.

Ask within, why did this happen *for* me?

If you're meant to suffer, then you are also meant to overcome this and be free. What will that freedom feel like? What can you do right now to get there from where you stand?

Try these transformative statements and fill in the blanks to help life begin to work *for* you:

My disappointments are teaching me to _____.

My suffering and pain is teaching me the way to _____.

My resentment is teaching me how to _____.

My grief is showing me how to _____.

My guilt is teaching me _____.

My jealousy is giving me the tools to _____.

My adversity is showing me how to _____.

The Universe wants to help you grow and sometimes that growth must come through the pathway of adversity and defeat. No human being is exempt.

The key to exponential growth is to welcome the adversity and defeat and use it as a tool to help you get through anything.

When you believe life is happening *for* you, you become capable and strong. You take charge of your reactions to life instead of your reactions taking charge of you. You move from being a victim of your circumstances to becoming master of your reaction to those circumstances.

Invoke faith that adversity and defeat are providing you the exact tools to know success in the exact way you need to learn it.

Congratulations, you now possess the golden tool to persevere and prevail when everything around you goes wrong.

You are at a critical choice point.

Will you continue to see events, people, and things in your life as happening *to* you or *for* you?

What's it going to be?

If you decide that life is now happening *for* you, let's move on to Question 4.

Question 4: How do I Apply this Learning and Teaching?

As you come to terms with Question 3, you must put the teaching lesson into play. Positive action is required to complete the circle of learning.

How do you create positive action?

What is the positive replacement for the negative energy that you feel in this situation?

Find the good by practicing gratitude

You find the good in that person, situation, or circumstance, no matter how small or trivial it may seem.

Try this. Name five things you are grateful for.

Note how you feel after you say the five things.

If you want to go further, here is a day-long action plan exercise. Fill in these blanks and focus on them for one full day in all of your interactions, including with your family, friends, and at the office.

Once you complete one full day, apply the *practicing gratitude* statements to everything and everyone for one full week.

Once you finish one full week, take this exercise a step further and apply these statements to everything and everyone for three full weeks.

I recommend setting aside time first thing in the morning to focus on finding the good by practicing gratitude, and also at the end of the day as the last thing you do before going to sleep.

Practicing Gratitude:

The gratitude I have for my partner or spouse today is: ___ .

The gratitude I have for my team is: _____ .

The gratitude I have for my boss is: _____ .

The gratitude I have for my family is: _____ .

The gratitude I have for the person I have constant conflict with is:

_____ .

The gratitude I have for myself is: _____ .

The gratitude I have for _____ is: ____ .

When you focus on the good in life in gratitude, the good will automatically find you. You can turn adversity and defeat into your greatest asset with a plan of positive action.

Start now by *finding the good* in everything.
Gratitude is just waiting to take you places you've never been.
Start your journey now!

ABOUT THE AUTHORS

Timothy Chhim

Timothy is a motivational speaker and owner of an Allstate Insurance Agency in Nanuet, New York, USA. He was born in a rural village in Cambodia and from a young age dreamed of freedom and a better life. When the communist Khmer Rouge, under the leadership of Pol Pot, seized power in 1975, Timothy was among thousands who were forced to leave the capital city of Phnom Penh. He was singled out as an educated citizen as well as a Republic official, having served as a police officer, and was sent to the jungle to be killed. He managed to escape, after many failed attempts, and survived to reach the safety of Thailand and later the USA.

Tom Cunningham

Tom is a motivational speaker, radio host, and life coach. He was diagnosed with Rheumatoid Arthritis at the age of five, a disease that affects every joint in his body, causing constant pain and making many day-to-day activities challenging. He has been in the hospital over 40 times for arthritis flare-ups and surgeries. In addition, high doses of the steroid prednisone stunted his growth, and he stands 5'1" tall. Despite the pain and challenges that come from living with Rheumatoid Arthritis, Tom chooses a positive mental attitude, and answers "Amazing!" to anyone who asks how he is. Tom and his wife, Kim, live in Brampton, Ontario, Canada. http://www.tom2tall.com/Law-of-Success.html

Taylor Tagg

Taylor Tagg is a published author, professional speaker, and radio show host. He has written three personal growth books, *Enrich Your Sunrise, The Path to a Peaceful Heart,* and co-authored *Adversity to Advantage.* Taylor's podcast, *Journey to Success,* showcases people who are passionate about making a difference in the world with transformational businesses and ideas. Taylor's natural talent lies in coaching people to fulfill their emotional and spiritual potential. As a Forgiveness Champion and Emotional Intelligence Coach, Taylor empowers those dealing with significant adversity to aspire to peace using his proven process. He lives in Memphis, Tennessee with his wife Sherri. http://www.theevolvingheart.com/

A FINAL WORD

We (Tim, Tom, and Taylor) thank you for reading Adversity to Advantage. We have open-heartedly shared our stories of suffering with you, so that you may be inspired to turn your life's obstacles into opportunity.

Although we faced many different enemies, our journeys share a common thread of struggling with fear, helplessness, and ultimately experiencing triumph.

And now you are a part of the *Adversity to Advantage Family.* We look forward to hearing about your story of transformation and seeing you on the road to victory.

We are with you every step of the way.

Please join us and share your story of overcoming adversity at the Adversity to Advantage community adversitytoadvantagebook.com

ADVERSITY TO ADVANTAGE COACHING

Passionate about serving others, we (Tim, Tom, and Taylor) are ready to help you triumph over the unimaginable adversity in your life.

A2A Coaching Packages are available for those who want specific guidance, emotional support, and hands on strategies to put the past behind you and embrace the bright future ahead.

Thank you for being a part of the *Adversity to Advantage Family.* We look forward to serving you soon and hearing about your story of transformation.

Please visit adversitytoadvantagebook.com to schedule time with Tim, Tom, and Taylor and book them to speak at your next inspirational event.

Printed in Great Britain
by Amazon

18972950R00061

CW00349984

65

AND
PROUD
OF IT

summersdale

65 AND PROUD OF IT

Summersdale Publishers Ltd
46 West Street
Chichester
West Sussex
PO19 1RP
UK

www.summersdale.com

Printed and bound in the Czech Republic

ISBN: 978-1-84953-693-6

Substantial discounts on bulk quantities of Summersdale books are available to corporations, professional associations and other organisations. For details contact Nicky Douglas by telephone: +44 (0) 1243 756902, fax: +44 (0) 1243 786300 or email: nicky@summersdale.com.

TO...

FROM.....................................

CONTENTS

ANOTHER
YEAR
OLDER

OLD AGE IS CATCHING
UP WITH ME, OR AM I
CATCHING UP WITH IT?

Stanley Victor Paskavich

SO MAYST THOU LIVE,
DEAR! MANY YEARS, IN
ALL THE BLISS THAT
LIFE ENDEARS.

Thomas Hood

I'M 65... BUT IF THERE
WERE 15 MONTHS IN
EVERY YEAR, I'D
ONLY BE 48.

James Thurber

WHENEVER THE TALK
TURNS TO AGE, I SAY I'M
49 PLUS VAT.

Lionel Blair

EVENTUALLY YOU
WILL REACH A POINT IN
LIFE WHEN YOU STOP
LYING ABOUT YOUR AGE
AND START BRAGGING
ABOUT IT.

Will Rogers

THE BEST
BIRTHDAYS OF
ALL ARE THOSE
THAT HAVEN'T
ARRIVED YET.

Robert Orben

I ABSOLUTELY REFUSE
TO REVEAL MY AGE.
WHAT AM I — A CAR?

Cyndi Lauper

SOME PEOPLE REACH
THE AGE OF 60
BEFORE OTHERS.

Samuel Hood

GROW OLD ALONG
WITH ME!
THE BEST IS
YET TO BE.

Robert Browning

EVERY YEAR ON YOUR
BIRTHDAY, YOU GET A
CHANCE TO START NEW.

Sammy Hagar

WE ARE ALWAYS THE SAME AGE INSIDE.

Gertrude Stein

OUR BIRTHDAYS ARE
FEATHERS IN THE BROAD
WING OF TIME.

Jean Paul

MY, MY, 65! I GUESS
THIS MARKS THE FIRST
DAY OF THE REST OF OUR
LIFE SAVINGS.

Anonymous

YOU CAN'T TURN BACK
THE CLOCK, BUT YOU CAN
WIND IT UP AGAIN.

Bonnie Prudden

SIXTY IS THE
NEW FORTY!

Bill Maher

JUST
WHAT
I ALWAYS
WANTED

YOU KNOW YOU'RE
GETTING OLD WHEN THE
CANDLES COST MORE
THAN THE CAKE.

Bob Hope

GOD GAVE US THE GIFT
OF LIFE; IT IS UP TO US
TO GIVE OURSELVES THE
GIFT OF LIVING WELL.

Voltaire

HER BIRTHDAY'S
OUR FETE DAY,
WE'LL MAKE IT
OUR GREAT DAY,
AND GIVE HER
OUR PRESENTS
AND SING HER
OUR SONG.

E. Nesbit

WHY IS BIRTHDAY CAKE
THE ONLY FOOD YOU CAN
SPIT ON AND BLOW ON
AND EVERYBODY RUSHES
TO GET A PIECE?

Bobby Kelton

A HUG IS THE PERFECT GIFT; ONE SIZE FITS ALL, AND NOBODY MINDS IF YOU EXCHANGE IT.

Anonymous

EVERY BIRTHDAY, EVERY
CELEBRATION ENDS WITH
SOMETHING SWEET,
A CAKE, AND PEOPLE
REMEMBER. IT'S ALL
ABOUT THE MEMORIES.

Buddy Valastro

IF INSTEAD OF A
GEM, OR EVEN A
FLOWER, WE SHOULD
CAST THE GIFT OF A
LOVING THOUGHT INTO
THE HEART OF A FRIEND,
THAT WOULD BE GIVING
AS THE ANGELS GIVE.

George MacDonald

THERE ARE 364 DAYS
WHEN YOU MIGHT
GET UN-BIRTHDAY
PRESENTS... AND ONLY
ONE FOR BIRTHDAY
PRESENTS, YOU KNOW.

Lewis Carroll

A GIFT, WITH A KIND
COUNTENANCE, IS A
DOUBLE PRESENT.

Proverb

NOBODY CAN BE
UNCHEERED WITH
A BALLOON.

A. A. Milne

GRIN
AND
BEAR
IT

LIVE YOUR LIFE
AND FORGET
YOUR AGE.

Norman Vincent Peale

GET READY FOR THE
65-YEAR-OLD SHUFFLE:
SHUFFLING ALONG,
SHUFFLING CARDS, AND
PLAYING SHUFFLEBOARD.

Greg Tamblyn

I DON'T KNOW HOW
I GOT OVER THE HILL
WITHOUT GETTING
TO THE TOP.

Will Rogers

'AGE' IS THE
ACCEPTANCE OF A
TERM OF YEARS. BUT
MATURITY IS THE
GLORY OF YEARS.

Martha Graham

AT MY AGE
'GETTING LUCKY'
MEANS FINDING MY CAR
IN THE PARKING LOT.

Anonymous

I DON'T WANT TO RETIRE.
I'M NOT THAT GOOD AT
CROSSWORD PUZZLES.

Norman Mailer

I REFUSE TO ADMIT I'M
MORE THAN 52, EVEN
IF THAT DOES MAKE MY
SONS ILLEGITIMATE.

Nancy Astor

OLD AGE IS AN
EXCELLENT TIME FOR
OUTRAGE. MY GOAL IS
TO SAY OR DO AT LEAST
ONE OUTRAGEOUS THING
EVERY WEEK.

Maggie Kuhn

AGE IS AN ISSUE
OF MIND OVER
MATTER. IF YOU
DON'T MIND, IT
DOESN'T MATTER.

Mark Twain

I SO ENJOY WAKING
UP AND NOT HAVING
TO GO TO WORK. SO I
DO IT THREE OR FOUR
TIMES A DAY.

Gene Perret

IT'S SAD TO GROW OLD, BUT NICE TO RIPEN.

Brigitte Bardot

NO MATTER WHAT
HAPPENS, I'M LOUD,
NOISY, EARTHY AND
READY FOR MUCH
MORE LIVING.

Elizabeth Taylor

STOP WORRYING ABOUT
THE POTHOLES IN THE
ROAD AND CELEBRATE
THE JOURNEY!

Anonymous

I'M NOT INTERESTED IN AGE... YOU'RE AS OLD AS YOU FEEL.

Elizabeth Arden

DO A
LITTLE
DANCE,
MAKE A
LITTLE
LOVE

LET US CELEBRATE THE
OCCASION WITH WINE
AND SWEET WORDS.

Plautus

THE AGEING PROCESS
HAS YOU FIRMLY IN ITS
GRASP IF YOU NEVER
GET THE URGE TO
THROW A SNOWBALL.

Doug Larson

I'M TOO OLD TO DO
THINGS BY HALF.

Lou Reed

51

I CELEBRATE MYSELF,
AND SING MYSELF.

Walt Whitman

IT'S IMPORTANT TO
HAVE A TWINKLE IN
YOUR WRINKLE.

Anonymous

TO ME, OLD AGE IS
ALWAYS 15 YEARS
OLDER THAN I AM.

Bernard Baruch

THE OTHER DAY A MAN
ASKED ME WHAT I
THOUGHT WAS THE BEST
TIME OF LIFE. 'WHY,' I
ANSWERED WITHOUT A
THOUGHT, 'NOW.'

David Grayson

I ALWAYS MAKE A POINT
OF STARTING THE
DAY AT 6 A.M. WITH
CHAMPAGNE. IT GOES
STRAIGHT TO THE HEART
AND CHEERS ONE UP.

John Mortimer

IT'S TIME TO START LIVING THE LIFE YOU'VE IMAGINED.

Henry James

LIFE IS TOO SHORT, SO
KISS SLOWLY, LAUGH
INSANELY, LOVE TRULY
AND FORGIVE QUICKLY.

Anonymous

LIFE IS JUST ONE GRAND, SWEET SONG, SO START THE MUSIC.

Ronald Reagan

WITH MIRTH AND
LAUGHTER LET OLD
WRINKLES COME.

William Shakespeare

DON'T WAIT. MAKE MEMORIES TODAY. CELEBRATE YOUR LIFE!

Anonymous

YOUNG
AT
HEART

RETIREMENT AT 65 IS RIDICULOUS. WHEN I WAS 65 I STILL HAD PIMPLES.

George Burns

IT'S NOT HOW OLD
YOU ARE, BUT HOW
YOU ARE OLD.

Marie Dressler

YOUTH HAS NO AGE.

Pablo Picasso

A MAN GROWING OLD BECOMES A CHILD AGAIN.

Sophocles

YOU'RE ONLY YOUNG
ONCE, BUT YOU CAN
ALWAYS BE IMMATURE.

Dave Barry

AGE MERELY SHOWS
WHAT CHILDREN
WE REMAIN.

Johann Wolfgang von Goethe

ANOTHER BELIEF OF
MINE: THAT EVERYONE
ELSE MY AGE IS AN
ADULT, WHEREAS I AM
MERELY IN DISGUISE.

Margaret Atwood

I'M HAPPY TO REPORT
THAT MY INNER CHILD
IS STILL AGELESS.

James Broughton

YOUTHFULNESS
IS ABOUT HOW YOU
LIVE, NOT WHEN YOU
WERE BORN.

Karl Lagerfeld

TO STOP
AGEING, KEEP
ON RAGING.

Michael Forbes

ALL WOULD LIVE LONG, BUT NONE WOULD BE OLD.

Benjamin Franklin

WHEN IT COMES
TO STAYING YOUNG,
A MINDLIFT BEATS
A FACELIFT ANY DAY.

Marty Bucella

MEN CHASE GOLF
BALLS WHEN THEY'RE
TOO OLD TO CHASE
ANYTHING ELSE.

Groucho Marx

THERE ARE PEOPLE
WHOSE WATCH STOPS AT A
CERTAIN HOUR AND WHO
REMAIN PERMANENTLY
AT THAT AGE.

Charles Augustin Sainte-Beuve

IN THE MIDST OF
WINTER, I FINALLY
LEARNED THAT
THERE WAS IN ME AN
INVINCIBLE SUMMER.

Albert Camus

I WILL NEVER GIVE
INTO OLD AGE UNTIL
I BECOME OLD. AND I'M
NOT OLD YET!

Tina Turner

THE ABILITY TO
LAUGH, ESPECIALLY AT
OURSELVES, KEEPS THE
HEART LIGHT AND THE
MIND YOUNG.

Anonymous

YOU'RE ONLY AS YOUNG
AS THE LAST TIME YOU
CHANGED YOUR MIND.

Timothy Leary

OLDER
AND
WISER?

THE MORE SAND
HAS ESCAPED FROM
THE HOURGLASS OF OUR
LIFE, THE CLEARER
WE SHOULD SEE
THROUGH IT.

Jean Paul

THE FIRST SIGN OF
MATURITY IS THE
DISCOVERY THAT THE
VOLUME KNOB ALSO
TURNS TO THE LEFT.

Jerry M. Wright

ONE OF THE GOOD
THINGS ABOUT
GETTING OLDER IS YOU
FIND YOU'RE MORE
INTERESTING THAN
MOST OF THE PEOPLE
YOU MEET.

Lee Marvin

THE MAN OF WISDOM IS
THE MAN OF YEARS.

Edward Young

LIFE CAN ONLY BE
UNDERSTOOD BACKWARDS;
BUT IT MUST BE LIVED
FORWARDS.

Søren Kierkegaard

OLD AGE IS READY
TO UNDERTAKE TASKS
THAT YOUTH SHIRKED
BECAUSE THEY WOULD
TAKE TOO LONG.

W. Somerset Maugham

AS WE GROW OLDER, OUR BODIES GET SHORTER AND OUR ANECDOTES LONGER.

Robert Quillen

IF I HAD MY LIFE TO
LIVE OVER AGAIN,
I'D MAKE THE SAME
MISTAKES, ONLY SOONER.

Tallulah Bankhead

YOUTH IS THE TIME FOR
ADVENTURES OF THE
BODY, BUT AGE FOR THE
TRIUMPHS OF THE MIND.

Logan Pearsall Smith

AUTUMN IS THE
MELLOWER SEASON,
AND WHAT WE LOSE IN
FLOWERS, WE MORE
THAN GAIN IN FRUITS.

Samuel Butler

IF YOU ARE 60 YEARS
OLD AND YOU HAVE
NO REGRETS, YOU
HAVEN'T LIVED.

Christy Moore

THE OLDER I GROW THE
MORE I DISTRUST THE
FAMILIAR DOCTRINE THAT
AGE BRINGS WISDOM.

H. L. Mencken

THE WHITER MY HAIR
BECOMES, THE MORE
READY PEOPLE ARE TO
BELIEVE WHAT I SAY.

Bertrand Russell

I'VE REACHED AN
AGE WHEN I CAN'T
USE MY YOUTH AS
AN EXCUSE FOR MY
IGNORANCE ANY MORE.

Helen-Janet Bonellie

AS YOU GROW OLDER,
YOU WILL DISCOVER THAT
YOU HAVE TWO HANDS,
ONE FOR HELPING
YOURSELF, THE OTHER
FOR HELPING OTHERS.

Audrey Hepburn

A HEALTHY OLD FELLOW, WHO IS NOT A FOOL, IS THE HAPPIEST CREATURE LIVING.

Richard Steele

ITS GOLDEN RICHNESS
SPEAKS NOT OF
THE INNOCENCE OF
SPRING... BUT OF THE
MELLOWNESS AND
KINDLY WISDOM OF
APPROACHING AGE.

Lin Yutang on autumn

BORN TO BE WILD —
LIVE TO OUTGROW IT.

Douglas Horton

EXPERIENCE IS A
COMB THAT LIFE GIVES
YOU AFTER YOU LOSE
YOUR HAIR.

Judith Stern

AGEING SEEMS TO BE THE ONLY AVAILABLE WAY TO LIVE A LONG LIFE.

Kitty O'Neill Collins

LIVE, LOVE AND LAST

YOU CAN ONLY PERCEIVE REAL BEAUTY IN A PERSON AS THEY GET OLDER.

Anouk Aimée

THE SECRET TO
STAYING YOUNG IS TO
LIVE HONESTLY, EAT
SLOWLY AND LIE ABOUT
YOUR AGE.

Lucille Ball

AGE ISN'T HOW OLD YOU ARE BUT HOW OLD YOU FEEL.

Gabriel García Márquez

CHERISH ALL YOUR
HAPPY MOMENTS; THEY
MAKE A FINE CUSHION
FOR OLD AGE.

Christopher Morley

ALTHOUGH IT SOUNDS
ABSURD, IT IS TRUE TO
SAY I FELT YOUNGER AT
60 THAN I FELT AT 20.

Ellen Glasgow

THE KEY TO SUCCESSFUL
AGEING IS TO PAY AS
LITTLE ATTENTION TO
IT AS POSSIBLE.

Judith Regan

MEN DO NOT QUIT
PLAYING BECAUSE THEY
GROW OLD; THEY GROW
OLD BECAUSE THEY
QUIT PLAYING.

Oliver Wendell Holmes Jr

I'M GROWING OLD; I DELIGHT IN THE PAST.

Henri Matisse

MY ADVICE FOR LIFE:
DANCE AND SING YOUR
SONG WHILE THE PARTY
IS STILL ON.

Rasheed Ogunlaru

HE DRANK TO LIFE, TO
ALL IT HAD BEEN, TO
WHAT IT WAS, TO WHAT
IT WOULD BE.

Sean O'Casey

PEOPLE SAY I'M INTO
MY SECOND CHILDHOOD.
THE REALITY IS THAT
I NEVER LEFT MY
FIRST ONE.

Spike Milligan

THE GOOD OLD DAYS
ARE NOW.

Tom Clancy

I LOVE EVERYTHING
THAT'S OLD: OLD
FRIENDS, OLD TIMES,
OLD MANNERS, OLD
BOOKS, OLD WINES.

Oliver Goldsmith

AGE IS JUST A STATE
OF MIND, AND YOU ARE
AS OLD AS YOU THINK
YOU ARE.

Abhishek Bachchan

ILLS,
PILLS
AND
TWINGES

I DON'T DO ALCOHOL
ANY MORE — I GET THE
SAME EFFECT JUST
STANDING UP FAST.

Anonymous

I DON'T FEEL OLD.
I DON'T GENERALLY
FEEL ANYTHING UNTIL
NOON, THEN IT'S TIME
FOR MY NAP.

Bob Hope

I USED TO THINK
I'D LIKE LESS GREY
HAIR. NOW I'D LIKE
MORE OF IT.

Richie Benaud

I'LL KEEP SWIVELLING
MY HIPS UNTIL THEY
NEED REPLACING.

Tom Jones

JUST
REMEMBER,
ONCE YOU'RE
OVER THE HILL
YOU BEGIN TO
PICK UP SPEED.

Charles M. Schulz

THE EASIEST WAY
TO DIMINISH THE
APPEARANCE OF
WRINKLES IS TO KEEP
YOUR GLASSES OFF
WHEN YOU LOOK IN
THE MIRROR.

Joan Rivers

EACH YEAR IT GROWS
HARDER TO MAKE ENDS
MEET – THE ENDS I
REFER TO ARE HANDS
AND FEET.

Richard Armour

AGE SELDOM ARRIVES
SMOOTHLY OR QUICKLY.
IT'S MORE OFTEN A
SUCCESSION OF JERKS.

Jean Rhys

OLDER PEOPLE
SHOULDN'T EAT HEALTH
FOOD, THEY NEED ALL
THE PRESERVATIVES
THEY CAN GET.

Robert Orben

YOU DON'T KNOW REAL
EMBARRASSMENT UNTIL
YOUR HIP SETS OFF A
METAL DETECTOR.

Ross McGuinness

THEY SAY THAT AGE IS
ALL IN YOUR MIND. THE
TRICK IS KEEPING IT
FROM CREEPING DOWN
INTO YOUR BODY.

Anonymous

I DON'T PLAN TO GROW
OLD GRACEFULLY. I PLAN
TO HAVE FACELIFTS
UNTIL MY EARS MEET.

Rita Rudner

I'M AT AN AGE WHEN
MY BACK GOES OUT
MORE THAN I DO.

Phyllis Diller

I HAVE EVERYTHING
I HAD 20 YEARS AGO,
ONLY IT'S ALL A LITTLE
BIT LOWER.

Gypsy Rose Lee

AS YOU GET OLDER
THREE THINGS HAPPEN.
THE FIRST IS YOUR
MEMORY GOES, AND I
CAN'T REMEMBER THE
OTHER TWO...

Norman Wisdom

EVERYTHING SLOWS
DOWN WITH AGE, EXCEPT
THE TIME IT TAKES
CAKE AND ICE CREAM TO
REACH YOUR HIPS.

John Wagner

MY DOCTOR TOLD ME
TO DO SOMETHING
THAT PUTS ME OUT OF
BREATH, SO I'VE TAKEN
UP SMOKING AGAIN.

Jo Brand

GRANT ME CHASTITY AND CONTINENCE, BUT NOT YET.

Augustine of Hippo

I HAVE A FURNITURE
PROBLEM. MY CHEST
HAS FALLEN INTO
MY DRAWERS.

Billy Casper

I'VE ONLY GOT ONE
WRINKLE AND I'M
SITTING ON IT.

Jeanne Calment

LET US RESPECT GREY
HAIRS, ESPECIALLY
OUR OWN.

J. P. Sears

I AM GETTING TO AN AGE
WHEN I CAN ONLY ENJOY
THE LAST SPORT LEFT. IT
IS CALLED HUNTING FOR
YOUR SPECTACLES.

Edward Grey

TIME MAY BE A GREAT
HEALER, BUT IT'S A
LOUSY BEAUTICIAN.

Anonymous

LOOKING 50 IS GREAT —
IF YOU'RE 60.

Joan Rivers

NATURE DOES NOT
EQUALLY DISTRIBUTE
ENERGY. SOME PEOPLE
ARE BORN OLD AND TIRED
WHILE OTHERS ARE
GOING STRONG AT 70.

Dorothy Thompson

THE THREE AGES OF
MAN: YOUTH, MIDDLE
AGE, AND 'MY WORD,
YOU DO LOOK WELL'.

June Whitfield

143

IF WRINKLES MUST
BE WRITTEN ON OUR
BROWS, LET THEM NOT
BE WRITTEN UPON
THE HEART.

James A. Garfield

CHIN UP,
UP,
CHEST
OUT

I DON'T BELIEVE IN
AGEING. I BELIEVE IN
FOREVER ALTERING
ONE'S ASPECT TO
THE SUN.

Virginia Woolf

ANYONE WHO KEEPS THE
ABILITY TO SEE BEAUTY
NEVER GROWS OLD.

Franz Kafka

GROWING OLD IS NO
MORE THAN A BAD HABIT
WHICH A BUSY MAN HAS
NO TIME TO FORM.

André Maurois

THE OLD BEGIN TO
COMPLAIN OF THE
CONDUCT OF THE
YOUNG WHEN THEY
THEMSELVES ARE NO
LONGER ABLE TO SET A
BAD EXAMPLE.

François de la Rochefoucauld

WHEN YOU ARE
DISSATISFIED AND
WOULD LIKE TO GO BACK
TO YOUR YOUTH, THINK
OF ALGEBRA.

Will Rogers

WHATEVER WITH
THE PAST HAS GONE,
THE BEST IS ALWAYS
YET TO COME.

Lucy Larcom

I'M NOT 60, I'M 'SEXTY'!

Dolly Parton

EVERYONE IS THE AGE OF THEIR HEART.

Guatemalan proverb

AGE IS AN OPPORTUNITY NO LESS THAN YOUTH ITSELF.

Henry Wadsworth Longfellow

NICE TO BE HERE?
AT MY AGE IT'S NICE
TO BE ANYWHERE.

George Burns

FROM OUR BIRTHDAY,
UNTIL WE DIE,
IS BUT THE WINKING
OF AN EYE.

W. B. Yeats

IF YOU ASSOCIATE
ENOUGH WITH OLDER
PEOPLE... YOU WILL
GAIN A SENSE OF
CONTINUITY AND OF THE
POSSIBILITIES FOR A
FULL LIFE.

Margaret Mead

YOU ARE NEVER TOO
OLD TO SET ANOTHER
GOAL OR TO DREAM
A NEW DREAM.

C. S. Lewis

WE TURN NOT OLDER WITH YEARS, BUT NEWER EVERY DAY.

Emily Dickinson

Meet Esme!

Our feathered friend Esme loves finding perfect quotes for the perfect occasion, and is almost as good at collecting them as she is at collecting twigs for her nest. She's always full of joy and happiness, singing her messages of goodwill in this series of uplifting, heart-warming books.

Follow Esme on Twitter at **@EsmeTheBird**.

For more information about our books, find us on Facebook at **Summersdale Publishers** and follow us on Twitter at **@Summersdale**.

www.summersdale.com

Table A20.4: Score for PRISM III variables

A. Cardiovascular / Neurologic vital signs

Systolic blood pressure MmHg

	Score = 3	Score = 7
Neonate		
Infant	40-55	< 40
Child	45-65	< 45
Adolescent	55-75	< 55
Else score = 0	65-85	< 65

Temperature

All ages	Score = 3
Else score = 0	< 33^{0}C (91.4^{0}F)
	or > 40^{0}C (104.^{0}F)

Mental Status

All ages	Score = 5
Else score = 0	Stupor/coma (GCS < 8)

Heart rate (bpm)

	Score = 3	Score = 4
Neonate		
Infant	215-225	> 225
Child	215-225	> 225
Adolescent	185-205	> 205
Else score = 0	145-155	> 155

Pupillary reflexes

	Score = 7	Score = 11
All ages	One fixed	Both fixed
Else score = 0		+ one reactive

B. Acid based blood gases

pH or total CO_2-mmol/L

	Score = 2	Score = 6	Score = 3
All ages	pH 7.0-7.28	pH < 7.0	pH > 7.55
	or pH 7.48-7.55	or	
Else score = 0	or total CO_2	total CO_2 < 5	

$PaCO_2$ (mmHg)

	Score = 1	Score = 3
All ages	50.0-75.0	> 75.0
Else score = 0		

PaO_2 (mmHg)

	Score = 3	Score = 6
All ages	42.0-49.9	< 42.0
Else score = 0		

C. Chemistry Tests

Glucose (see dataset)

All ages	Score = 2
Else score = 0	> 200 mg/dl (11.0 mmolL)

Potassium (see dataset)

All ages	Score = 3
Else score = 0	> 6.9 mmolL or mEq/L

Contd.